SOCIOLOGY OF LEGAL PROFESSION, LAW AND LEGAL SYSTEM :
The Indian Setting

SOCIOLOGY OF LEGAL PROFESSION, LAW AND LEGAL SYSTEM : The Indian Setting

DR. J.S. GANDHI

With a Foreword by
JUSTICE D.A. DESAI

GYAN PUBLISHING HOUSE
New Delhi - 110002

SOCIOLOGY OF LEGAL PROFESSION, LAW AND LEGAL SYSTEM :

The Indian Setting

ISBN :9788121200790

Published in 2015 in India by
Gyan Publishing House
23, Ansari Road, Daryaganj,
New Delhi - 110002
Phones : 23261060, 23282060 Fax : 23285914
e-mail : books@gyanbooks.com
website : gyanbooks.com

Laser Typesetting at : Vinayak Printers, Delhi
Printed at : Salasar Imaging System, Delhi

Dedicated to the Sacred Memory
of My Grandparents :
S. Shorie Singh
and
Mrs. Amrit Kaur

FOREWORD

LAW, lawyers, organised legal profession, law reform and allied subjects have recently been the subject matter of fascinating study, the contribution coming from such diverse sources as outstanding academics and sociologists (the author Dr. J.S. Gandhi, a sociologist), Judges and even consumers of justice. The divergence of opinion in the matter of evaluation, appraisal and social and professional accountability of the profession to the society and of the individual to his client is almost unbridgeable. Consequently, it varies from inaudible appreciation to strident criticism. The profession has acquired high visibility right from the time its noteworthy contribution in the framing of the Constitution because of 'its professionally ingrained forensic capability' which discloses the utilitarian side of the legal profession to the political parties on the ground that they are 'the best spokesmen for their policies—both inside and outside the Legislature. Their role, in selling their party's policies to the illiterate and semi-literate masses of the Indian society can hardly be over-emphasized' (page 8). Undoubtedly, since the independence even though legal profession is very adequately represented in the democratic political institutions like the Parliament and the State legislatures and even the Panchayats, to some extent the profession has lost its pre-eminence.

Since the independence while on one hand the share of the profession in the political power gradually diminished, its impact on the legal judicial system of the country proportionately shot up. Some of the stalwarts of the profession had their own social and econmic philosophy, howsoever loudly they proclaimed to the contrary, and, by their unquestioned forensic ability in the first phase, of the interpretation of the Constitution 1950-1967, they influenced the judicial thinking in such magnitude as to be able to weave in the same into the legal system by judicial pronouncement without judicial power and without any accountability to the society. This phenomenon needs to be analysed in the investigation of sociology of legal profession. One distinct advantage that the profession enjoys is that collectively it has no value system, no philosophy and individually there is no commitment to any particular set of values, the approach being *to plead the cause placed in your hands in the interest of the client* irrespective of the truth or otherwise of it or irrespective of the national good or national disaster that may emerge from the acceptance of the argument advanced for the client's cause. Justification is sought for this unsustainable position from a medieval cliche that the scoundrel must have a day in the court. And, in order to give him his day, he must be assisted by a member of the profession. The power of wealth has monopolised the best legal talent. The fall-out is that the profession as a whole has served the class interests of rising industrial capitalism and State capitalism in India.[1] In the misconceived concept of eqality before law, the rich employ the best talent and the poor because of his inability to pay for recognised talent, was assisted by equally poor talent, and the equality-oriented Judges tilted the balance in favour of the rich. The situation has become intolerable and needs analysis and examination. *Bhopal gas victims* vs. *U.C.C.* represents this cross culture.

The author from his *Lawyers and Touts* has gone into a more indepth study of the sociology of legal profession. He dealt with the legal aid scheme, as at present working, and almost exposed its inadequacy by pointing out that as a voluntary measure it has little chance of success in the present structure of the legal profession, when he describes the participation of the profession 'as a clever device by the profession for retaining control over the administration of the scheme ensuring maximum pay-off for its own members, rather than any genuine offer for the welfare of the poor and indigent.' (page 50).

Legal profession is monopolistic in character. Its collective strength acquired for itself a structural autonomy and succeeded in snatching 'peer's justice' jurisdiction to itself, without meaning any disrespect, with disastrous consequences. Numerous decisions in this behalf would shed light on this aspect which again needs an indepth study. Such instrospection should better come from the profession itself. The profession has also a vital role to play in the

1. U. Baxi : Sulakhani Devi Mahajan Memorial Lecture : Dec. 5, 1986-

matter of judicial appointments, law reforms, judicial reforms and removing road-blocks in access to justice. Little noteworthy has been attempted in this direction. However, as amongst the Judges, activists amongst lawyers are coming to the fore. In fact, the public interest litigation which has caught the eye of the people sorely in search of illusory justice, has been the handiwork of legal activists. While examining their 'phenomenology of emergent culture', the author refers to the work of numerous legal activists which has opened up new vistas for law as an instrument of social engineering.

I am sure the book, which once taken in hand cannot be set aside, would help in reforming the profession so as to make it a powerful instrument for translating into action the goal enshrined in Art. 39A of the Constitution.

D.A. DESAI

Chairman
Law Commission,
Government of India,
Shastri Bhawan, New Delhi

PREFACE

'LAW' indeed is a jealous mistress; and, I don't claim to be a very eligible suitor, either. All the same, its seduction over me has been ever-ensnaring and gripping over the years. Equipped merely with the little torch of sociology, I have been trying to find my way into various lanes and by-lanes, connecting profession with the society, judiciary and legal system, assessing their adequacies or otherwise vis-a-vis the massive social change mandated both constitutionally and politically. The fruit of all this engagement over the past twelve years or so is presented here through eight distinct chapters, which will test both a sociologist's penchant for rigour and a lawman's self-certitude and profoundity. And, upto all such hazards, I submit myself as a sacrificial goat.

More than half of these studies—especially those concerning lawyers and politics, the legal and professional culture, criminal justice etc., have benefitted enormously from the materials collected for the project *Lawyers and Their Social Concerns*, funded by the Ford Foundation, New Delhi. I am grateful to the foundation, for this research grant. In particular, I want to put on record my heart-felt thanks and gratitude to Mr. R. Sudarshan, Assistant Representative of the Foundation in Delhi and also to Dr. Carolyn Elliot, the ex-Programme Officer of the Foundation. My profound gratitude also remains to my senior colleague and teacher Prof. Yogendra Singh for his ever-inspiring and illuminating consultations. My secretary Miss Neelam Sharma has been of tremendous help in preparing the manuscript for publication in the shortest possible time.

Associate Professor
Centre for the Study of Social Systems,
Jawaharlal Nehru University,
New Delhi

J.S. GANDHI

CONTENTS

Chapter One

LAWYERS AND POLITY IN INDIA : HISTORICAL AND CONTEMPORARY CONTEXT

INTRODUCTION

THIS CHAPTER is purported to present an overall profile of relationship between lawyers and polity in the Indian society—both in its historical and contemporary perspective. The nature of this connection and inter-action has been changing over the years, but there are also some interesting continuities between the settings of British India and of modern India. In order to complete this picture, we have also found it necessary to extend our inquiry to the judges in the premier courts of the country – the High Courts and the Supreme Court of India. Judges, though not *professional* in the strict theoretical sense of the term, do play a very special role in patterning the contours of a polity—especially that of a developing ex-colonial society, through several innovative and creative interpretations of the *rational legal system,* enshrined in the Constitution according to their perceptions of the emergent needs of the people.

We shall therefore, pursue our inquiry in two parts. Part I will be concerned with lawyers and will take note of their political sensitivities and patterns of political participation both in the pre-independence and the post-independence contexts. Part II, on the other hand, will be specifically concerned with judges and will carry out the same exercise in similar contexts. Towards the end, we shall try to integrate the evidence from these two sections and attempt a composite statement on the nature of relationship between the legal profession and the polity.

PART I : LAWYERS

1. Pre-Independence Context : Growth of Socio-Political Sensitivity

Modern legal profession in the West has come a long way from its exclusive occupation with the protection and furtherance of the interests of the propertied class in the late nineteenth and early twentieth centuries, to an active concern with the problems of the poor and the indigent in the recent era. But so far as its participation and sharing in the overall political power is concerned, it has continued since its very emergence in the Western societies. There is a curious parallel between the predominance of lawyers in the Court of Star Chambers in Tudor England and the presence of more than two-third lawyers in the current American National Legislature. Such a tendency on the part of the legal profession to locate itself within the centrality of socio-political relevance is easy to understand once we appreciate the fact that lawyers have a specialized efficiency of understanding, interpreting and applying law to protect their own interests or of such groups and classes as they might choose to represent or align themselves with. The progressive increase in the social and political sensitivity of the Indian legal profession illustrates the strength of above formulation.

The massive participation of the Indian legal profession in the political affairs of the country all through the twentieth century can be seen to spill into their participation in the political decision-making of the contemporary India. The struggle for country's independence even though alive all through the nineteenth century following the 'mutiny' of 1857, came to acquire a significant proportion only towards the end of the nineteenth century. In 1885, Indian National Congress—which was later to pioneer the entire struggle for national independence, was formed with a barrister—W.C. Bonnerjee, as its first president. Other important leaders of the party at that time were also lawyers such as Pherozeshah Mehta, Telang, Chandavarkar and Ranade, all practitioners of the Bombay High Court.[1] All through the subsequent

1. C.E. Buckland, *Dictionary of Indian Biography*, Greenwood, 1906.

years of crystallization and development of the national struggle for independence as well as the growth and development of the Indian National Congress party, lawyers played an extremely important part and occupied prominent leadership positions. Names such as those of Bal Gangadhar Tilak, Lala Lajpat Rai, Moti Lal Nehru, Sardar Patel, Jawaharlal Nehru etc. are reminiscent of historic contributions rendered by the legal profession to the cause of the Indian independence. When the movement for National independence gathered strong momentum under the leadership of Mahatma Gandhi in the post-1920 phase, several lawyers and barristers with well established practice, gave up their lucrative careers to jump into the national mainstream. As he started his mammoth Champaran project for investigating into the exploitation of the Indian peasants by the British indigo planters, several lawyers interviewed as many as 22,000 peasants and recorded their experiences of exploitation. "This *satyagraha* broke the grip of the planter on the peasants of the area and proved to the country what great public service could be achieved by well-motivated lawyers working together for the cause of human rights".[2] Rajendra Prasad (the first President of the Independent India) describes the great effect this work had on the legal profession of that area.

> Most of us who joined Gandhiji in Champaran were lawyers and not one had joined him with the idea of giving up the profession. But when we started working in Champaran, our outlook changed. We found it impossible, once we had undertaken it, to go back to our avocations without completing the task in hand. People who went there for few days remained there for months. When we had finished the work in Champaran, we returned home with new ideas, a new courage and a new programme. . . We could feel and realize that if the public life of Bihar was to be at all effective, some of us

2. Samuel Schmitthener, "A sketch of the Development of the Lega Profession in India," *Law and Society Review*, III, 1-2 Nov., 1968—Feb. 1969 p. 379.

would have to devote ourselves to it to the exclusion of everything.[3]

Another notable theatre of active political participation on the part of the legal profession during days of national struggle for independence, was Punjab—a state in the north of India. In order to curb the growing popular discontent against the British, the latter brought forth Rowlatt Act of 1919 which tended to severely curtail some of the civic rights such as the right to hold assemblies and freedom of expression. Several lawyers from Amritsar and Lahore District Courts organized a strong popular protest against this act. Notable among these were barrister Saiffudin Kitchlew, Bau Kanhaiya Lal Bhatia, Mohammed Yasin, Mir Maqbool Mahmood. The first of the above mentioned along with a medical doctor Satya Pal forged the famous Hindu-Muslim front for registering the above protest. Both of them were arrested resulting in frayed tempers among the general public of Amritsar city, which invited the wrath of the British administration culminating in the massacre of peaceful gathering at Jallianwala Bagh in Amritsar. After this, the British unleashed a reign of terror and repression in Punjab, and among those who suffered a variety of indignities were members of the legal profession :

> Martial law was proclaimed in Amritsar and subsequently extended to other districts. General Dyer was appointed the Administrator of Amritsar on 15th April. The same day all shops were opened. Thus the hartal (strike) came to an end. The courts opened for the first time on 22nd April, 1919. Lawyers were punished for their real or alleged interest in politics, and on 23rd April they were enrolled as special constables, a step which had been taken as a vindictive measure. They were insulted and made to witness public flogging and to carry furniture like ordinary coolies. Their role call was held twice a day. They were relieved of their onerous duties on 12th

3. Rajendra Prasad, *Autobiography*, Bombay, Asia Publishing House 1957, p. 100.

May. (Reproduced from Gandhi, 1982).[4]

Besides spearheading the popular protest against the British, Indian lawyers also worked through the courts for rights and equality between Indians and Englishmen; and they gained membership and power in the provincial legislative councils and local municipalities—which were British experiments in giving limited autonomy to the Indian people.[5] It was in the vestibule of these civil-administrative bodies that the leadership which later came to play its important role in free India, acquired its first lessons in political and administrative realism. This complete dominance of lawyers in the municipal and provincial administration of the country was deeply resented by the British administration and also the pro-British Anglo-Indian population of India whereby this state of affairs came to be designated as *Vakil-raj* (lit. the rule of the lawyers).[6] How does one explain this deep involvement of the lawyers in the independence movement? A variety of factors seemed to have played their part in shaping this orientation of their's. First of all, their proficiency to deal with the British through the interpretation of their very laws gave them an honorific status among their own people, and a respectable status among the British. This fell in tune with natural demeanour and disposition of the aristocratic-fedual classes to which most of them had belonged for several generations. Secondly, as a careful reading of the memoirs of some of the leading leaders of the free India reveals, most of them clearly foresaw the imminence of the British withdrawal from India and thus a clear possibility that they might occupy the front-ranking positions in the political system of free India. All this is clearly revealed, for example, in the correspondence between Pandit Jawaharlal Nehru—the first Prime Minister of free India, and his father Pandit Moti Lal Nehru, a leading lawyer of his day. The latter exhorted his son

4. J.S. Gandhi, *Lawyers and Touts,* Hindustan Publishing Corporation, New Delhi, 1982.

5. Schmitthener, *op. cit.*

6. A.M.L. Fraser, *Among the Indian Rajas and Ryots*, London, Seeley and Company Ltd., 1912, p. 65.

to take to politics seriously assuring him that all what he would need by way of his economic maintenance would be easily available to him out of the earnings that he (Pandit Moti Lal Nehru) had made from his professional practice. A recent compilation of lawyers who participated in the independence movement shows that nearly half of the 184 lawyers listed by him, came to occupy important political positions—including ministerial positions in the free India.[7] All this urge for a conscious career-building came naturally to lawyers who have an in-built shrewedness to anticipate the turn of events and to watch their interests or of those whom they represent as counsels in a court of law.

2. Post-independence Context : Facing upto Systemic Change

(*a*) *Continuity and Departure* :

India freed itself from the British rule and lawyers opened their chapter of socio-political participation in Free India, by playing a formative and sheet-anchor role in constitution-making. Those who played probably the most significant role in outlining and shaping various contours of the constitution through their deliberations in the Constituent Assembly were nearly all lawyers, noteworthy among them being Pandit Jawaharlal Nehru (the first Prime Minister of Free India), Sardar Patel (the Home Minister in Pandit Nehru's cabinet), Dr. B.R. Ambedkar (later, Pandit Nehru's Law Minister) and Dr. Rajendra Prasad (the First President of Free India). A perusal of the proceedings of the Constituent Assembly (Rao, 1968) reveals clearly how some of the very basic percepts of the Indian Constitution such as *secularism, democracy, equalitarian-egalitarian* ideology were expounded,[8] elaborated and incorported by the lawyer-member of the Assembly. So fundamental was their contribution that even some of the well-known ambiguities in the Indian Constitution, such as the uncertainty regarding the primacy of the *fundamental rights* or the

7. Lalit Bhasin, *Lawyers in the Freedom Struggle of India*, Congress Centenary Celebration Committee, Delhi Art Press, Delhi, 1985.

8. B. Shiva Rao, *The Framing of India's Constitution*, Vols. I-V, The AIPP, New Delhi, 1968.

directive principles of state policy, owe their origin to the *formalistic* rather than *substantive-historic* expostulation of the Indian social reality on the part of the lawyers who adopted these terms for incorporation into the Indian Constitution.

Even after the Constitution was adopted, lawyers continued to play their important role in national politics. As Marc Galanter (1968-69) reports, lawyers constituted 35.3 per cent, 31.4 per cent, 30.0 per cent and 26.9 per cent of the total members, respectively in the first (1952-57), second (1957-62), third (1962-67) and fourth (1967-71) Lok Sabhas (i.e. National legislatures)[9] Galanter infers that the relative participation of the lawyers in the post-independence India, has gone down. This is not borne out by the nature of information available from the composition of the seventh Lok Sabha (1980-84). Seventh Lok Sabha, led by the Prime Minister Mrs. Indira Gandhi was sworn in March 1980[10] and was comprised of 527 members (out of a total scheduled membership of 544, since in 27 seats in different states, elections had yet to take place). A total of 168 members of parliament or 31.8 per cent of the total of 527 members were graduates in law. Further, out of this total 168 lawyers 121 or 72.02 per cent were in the ruling party (Cong. I) and the remaining *i.e.* 47 or 27.97 per cent were in opposition. Some more interesting facts regarding this Lok Sabha may also be noted. Mrs. Gandhi's cabinet in March 1980 was comprised of a total of 41 ministers including herself; out of this, lawyers accounted for 19 or 46.3 per cent of the total cabinet. Further, the top layer of her ministry *i.e.* comprising of the *cabinet rank* ministers, was constituted of 19 ministers, out of which 12 or 63 per cent were lawyers and were vested with such important portfolios as External Affairs, Finance, Agriculture, Information and Broadcasting, Law, Education etc. Another interesting inference which flows from the above figures is that the party in power *i.e.* Mrs. Gandhi-led Congress (I) had proportionately a higher percentage

9. Marc Galanter, "The Study of Indian Legal Profession", *Law and Society Review*, 111(2) : 201-17, 1968.

10. Who's Who : Lok Sabha, 1980.

of members of parliament (*i.e.* 121 out of its total strength of 351 or 34.4 per cent) from the legal profession as compared to the opposition (*i.e.* 47 out of its total strength of 176 or 26.7 per cent).

The situation in the latest—the eighth Lok Sabha is not any different. Rajiv Gandhi, the son of the previous Prime Minister Mrs. Indira Gandhi came to power in the beginning of 1985.[11] Out of the total of 512 members for whom the elections were held in the first instance, as many as 149 or 29.1 per cent were lawyers—123 or 24 per cent in the ruling Cong. (I) party and 24 or 4.6 per cent in the opposition. In the Cabinet (which is a three-tiered structure comprising of *Cabinet* ministers, *state* ministers, and *deputy* ministers), constituted for the first time after the elections, 25 out of 50 per cent were lawyers. Out of a total of 15 ministers of the *Cabinet rank* (*i.e.* the top-layer), 10 or 66.6 per cent were lawyers. Further, important portfolios such as Home Affairs, Education, Industry, Energy, Banking and Insurance, Information and Broadcasting etc. were put under the charge of the lawyer-members. Rajya Sabha or the *house of elders*, which is constituted of members elected both through indirect proportional representation and nomination is an ongoing body, with a regular cycle of replacements and consequent inflows of new members every year. Since, barring a few nominations, elections to all the positions are held on party-lines, rationale of fielding a candidate having a particular social or occupational background, on the part of a political party, can be similarly appreciated as for the Lok Sabha. An analysis of Rajya Sabha as it stood in 1984 (Who's Who 1985), reveals a preponderance of lawyers (33.47 per cent), agriculturists and teachers occupying the second and third positions with 15.5 per cent and 8.7 per cent respectively.

This lends an additional strength to our argument advanced above regarding Indian lawyer's propensity to acquire positions of political power by way of a conscious design and deliberate purpose. Their socio-political dominance of the pre-independence days has continued right into the post-independence era.

---

11. Who's Who : Lok Sabha, 1985.

But the pattern of profession's political participation which has emerged consequent upon the independence of the country is a distinct departure from its participation in the past. As against an "organized" involvement into the politics of the day by the general mass of profession.[12] during the independence movement, their participation in the post-independence era has been completely individual-based, directed by calculus of gains from aligning with a specific political party. On the other hand, for the political parties, who have been continuously drafting lawyers into their ranks, as apparent from their representation in the national legislature, it has indeed been a gainful proposition. This is so, because with their professionally ingrained forensic capabilities, the parties find in them the best spokesmen for their policies—both inside and outside the legislature. Their role, in selling their parties' policies to the illiterate and semi-literate masses of the Indian society can hardly be over-emphasized.

(*b*) *The Profession comes into Market :*

Inspired by incentive to participate in power-politics, and also conscious of their instrumentality to the political parties, the lawyers are now openly striving for political patronage and co-optation. One finds them, therefore, both in the *ruling party* as well as in the *opposition,* depending upon whichever party they feel will wield power in immediate or remote future. One finds them playing their professionally patented role of conscientious *brief-keeping* for whichever party or group they align themselves with. And, in keeping with their respective briefs, they have not been guided by considerations of professional values, propriety and professional rectitude. Often, they have upheld and pleaded against values they are expected to uphold as professional-keepers of law. I have carried out a qualitative content-analysis of such observations, remarks or comments as were made by lawyers—whether in the government or in opposition, concerning various components of the contemporary legal system in the country *i.e.* legal profession, judiciary or the current state of constitution, flaws in the legal system etc. All

12. Rajendra Prasad, *op. cit.*

these statements were reported in the national newspaper-media.* I have attempted this analysis for a restricted period of six years (*i.e.* from August 1975 to April 1981). Limited space does not permit me to report on the complete range of my findings. Therefore, I shall confine myself only to a small sampling of observations concerning some of the major issues which have figured in the public debates during this period. These will be reported separately for lawyers in the government and in the opposition.

(*c*) *Lawyers in the Government : their Perspectives :*

This category of lawyers made observations covering a wide range of issues and topics *i.e.* from those concerning the function of law in a democracy to those concerning the role of judiciary or of the Constitution *vis-a-vis* the changing social environment. The upshot of all these observations was to support the government and its policies, to try to condition and orient the legal profession or the judiciary to adopt a compliant attitude towards some constitutional departures being proposed by the government. They also encouraged both judges and lawyers to promote a certain 'thinking' or a 'philosophy' which was in tune with specific policy-formulations and policy-proposals.

(*i*) *The Hindu :* 26-9-1976

New Delhi, September 25. Inaugurating the new building of the High Court of Delhi, President of India, Mr. Fakhruddin A. Ahmed (himself having been a distinguished senior lawyer and former Advocate General of Assam) stressed that judiciary should assist the government in promoting the process of social change (summarised).

(*ii*) *The Sunday Standard* : 9-1-1977

Gwalior, January 8. Inaugurating the first *All India Judicial Officers' Conference*, organised by the Union Law Minister, Mr.

* Reference here is to such national dailies as Times of India, Statesman, Indian Express, Hindustan Times, Hindu. We have also drawn upon some important regional newspapers, such as Tribune, Ananda Bazar Patrika, Indian Observer.

H.R. Gokhale, today stressed the need for a change in the judicial system . . . The minister expressed the view that judges could not close their eyes to what was happening outside . . . that bringing administration of justice into concurrent list was also important. . . (which means pleading for bringing "justice" now a "state" subject into the joint purview of state and central government, and thus to plead for extending the power-radius of the central government).

(*iii*) *The Hindustan Times* : 26-7-1976

New Delhi, February 25. The Union Law Minister Mr. H.R. Gokhale feels that the power of the High Courts to issue writ so as to protect laws aimed at the socio-economic amelioration of the people. He said that the rule of the law would not be offended if the courts had no jurisdiction to declare *ultra vires* of the constitution, legislation passed by parliament.

(*iv*) *The Hindustan Times* : 27-2-1976

Calcutta, February 26. At the 1-day Conference of the West Bengal lawyers, Mr. H.R. Gokhale said that the provision for fundamental rights to property enshrined in the Constitution was totally irrelevant in so far as the common people of the country are concerned—(which means striking at the very basis of the Constitution of the country).

(*d*) *Pro-Government Legal Populism :*

Our analysis also brought out that in both the Congress and Janata Party regimes *i.e.* between 1975-80, lawyer-members of both the governments repeatedly engaged themselves in populistic statements and tactics with a view to bringing home to the public, government's "genuine" urge to carry out such changes in the existing legal systems as would make justice cheap and easily accessible. The ritual of appointing committees and sub-committees to consider such changes was invariably gone through. For example, note the following :—

The Hindu : 3-5-1979

New Delhi, May 2. A sub-committee of lawyer-MPs will

suggest to the government changes in the judicial system so that people could get speedy justice . . . The sub-committee will consist of Messrs . . . (all of whom are actively connected with the legal profession and thus had vested interests in the continuation of the present legal system).

Mrs. Gandhi-led Congress (I) came back to power in January 1980, and a declaration of the above type was made by her party too immediately thereafter. Thus one ruling party picked up where its predecessor, now a mere opposition party had left. Note the following report :—

Times of India : 8-2-1980

Hyderabad, February 7 (PTI). The Union Law Minister Mr. Shivashankar is considering the setting up of a 3-member committee to go into the question of judicial reforms. The Law Minister who was addressing a press conference here yesterday, made it clear that the matter would also be discussed with the Supreme Court "least we are blamed for interference with the judiciary". The minister said that the government was considering a scheme of barefoot lawyers—to appoint a law graduate for a group of 4 or 5 villages—so that he could go round and tell people what their rights were. He said this was also covered by the term "legal aid" as it did not merely mean defending a cause in the court.

A perusal of the professional activities of the lawyers—both within the government and outside, brings out another interesting *modus operandi* of legal populism on the part of lawyers in government. Under both the Janata and Congress (I) regimes (for the period under study), one often observed a conjuction between the politicians of the party-in-power on the one hand and members of the Bar or of the judiciary. In several public meetings organized by the lawyer practitioners and their organizations on issues and problems of contemporary relevance, leaders of the party-in-power participated and voiced their concern in the values of democracy, socialism and equality. Such opportunities provided legitimacy to both the profession and the politicians, since both could loudly profess their concern for the commonweal at these joint platforms. For the independent practitioners in particular, their effort in providing a professional platform to the politicians acted virtually as a good certificate for them to be moved into the inner corridors of power politics.

(*e*) *Lawyer—Judge—Politician Nexus* :

There is coming to the public view an increasing proximity between the lawyer on the one hand, and the politician and judge on the other. This is taking place especially at the higher professional levels *i.e.* for the lawyers practising at High Courts and at Supreme Court of India. The growing visibility of this phenomenon does incalculable damage to its public image and also underscores its incapacity to identify itself with the problems faced by the poor and the indigent clients, or with the issues of public interest in general. This professionally forbidden hobnobbing has been indentified and bemoaned by a famous legal-columnist Krishan Mahajan who writes his regular columns in one of the national dailies, *The Hindustan Times.* Writing under a saucy title "Dinner Lawyering" (*The Hindustan Times* : 10th October, 1983) he exposes this impropriety as follows :

> The latest in this damage is the dinner lawyering being indulged in by some influential seniors by inviting judges to their homes alongwith politicians and key government personnel. The judges of course are at fault in accepting such invitations because there is hardly a commodity, political or social issues, that is not pending before the court and a decision on which would not effect many of those attending the dinners. This becomes worse when the host senior lawyer is arguing cases in vital quarters before the judges invited. But the primary blame must go to the seniors for putting such a temptation before judges of rubbing shoulders with those in the executive and legislative wings. Once the seniors offer this opportunity to one set of jugdes they make it more difficult for the other sets of judges to decline such invitations and retain their value system of remaining aloof from the apparent advantage of such gathering.

The solution offered by Krishan Mahajan is that courts should de-institutionalize the distinctive status of "senior lawyers" as characterised by certain special privileges. But the malaise runs much deeper. There seems to have set in an all-round nemesis of the professional ethos manifested through all varieties of opportunistic endeavours with profit-making potentials. In view of the much expected and much-publicised 'role of the legal profession in the process of social change', one of the most promising measures with high potentials of stemming the rot is to tone up the functioning of professional bodies vesting them with certain jural-powers which may be used against deliberate professional defaulters. These professional bodies may also inculcate the requisite professional norms during the training and socialization of their members.

PART II : JUDGES

1 Native Judges and the colonial regime : The pre-independence context

As a part of involving the Indian elites into their system of administration, the British admitted them into the portals of higher education, including the legal education. As a consequence of this policy, starting about the beginning of 19th century, many Indians qualified as barristers and later practised in the presidency courts of Calcutta and Madras alongside their British counterparts. Not only that, some of the outstanding Indian lawyers were also invited to join on the bench, where they served with credit and distinction. An un-authored compilation of the biographical sketches of Indian Judges, reports as many as twenty one judges, all drawn from elite Hindu and Muslim families.[13] The service-careers of these judges, spanned approximately between the first quarter of the nineteenth century to the first quarter of the twentieth century. Their professional and public careers have been reported with lucidity though not completeness by their anonymous biographers in the source cited above. An inventory

13. *Indian Judges,* Biographical and Critical Sketches with Portraits, G.A. Natesan and Company, Madras, 1932.

of their public and political concerns—both before and after their careers on bench, shows, a wide-spectrum of 'moral' and 'political' views, a critique of British perspective on India and Indian society, exhorting them to rectify their lopsided view. While appreciating all these concerns of theirs as sampled in the following section, two facts must be kept in view. First : Indian movement for freedom from the British regime even though immanent and subdued in the popular protest all along the nineteenth century, became particularly manifest and politically organized only in the post-1920 phase when Mahatma Gandhi came back from South Africa to lead the freedom movement against the British in which several eminent lawyers of the day also joined. As such, strong political denunciation of the British system could not be expected as early as the beginning of the nineteenth century. Second, the intensity of invective with which the lawyers criticized the British system as well as the nature of activities in which they engaged themselves could not be expected from judges—especially in their post-bench phase, who had been conditioned to defend a *legally* constituted regime. Yet, we find in some cases, clear reflection of their political independence and even of 'patriotic' sentiments even though their plea is more to *rectify* the system than to *supplant* it. A few of such views and expressions, discerned as representative from a close reading of the above source are reproduced below.

We start with a sample of an unqualified commitment to the British and their rule in India :

> Loyalty to the British throne and Constitution is not only a virtue but its absence is a crime. I desire to impress upon you that loyalty to the British connection is the foundation on which India should be raised,
> (Sir, T. Muthuswami Ayyar (1832-1895), cited by his biographer from his private conversation in INDIAN JUDGES, New Delhi, 1932, p. 22).

It is easy to understand the motive force behind this gigantic faith in the vitality of the British rule, which many of Ayyar's mould nursed, once we recognize that the British were seen by them as epitomising the best in the Western civilization from which India could benefit, and such a faith with them sounded almost instinctive and automatic.

> There is something which makes me feel that the regeneration of India is a missson which the civilization of the West will accomplish (*Ibid.*).

This adoration seems all the more significant once we know that Sir Ayyar came from a caste (Brahmin) which is traditionally the repository of ancient religious beliefs and values with an uncompromising veneration for the scriptures, rituals and dogmas. Sir Ayyar's could therefore, be typical case of the conditioning of a traditional native personality by the values of Western legal system.

But the exultant admiration of Sir Muthuswami Ayyer for the British rule in India and his unqualified acceptance of Western civilization as a spring-source of Indian regeneration, can be contrasted with the attitude of another Brahmin, Sir Subramania Iyer, who succeeded the former as the judge of the Madras High Court. Both before and after his career as a judge, he played active role in public life. He was one of the founder-members of the Indian National Congress (founded in 1885, and later led the independence movement against the British rule, right upto 1947. When India became free), and was also a forceful leader of the famous Home Rule Movement started in 1917. He spared no words in criticising from the open public platforms, the arbitrary and exploitative character of the British regime in India. In his letter to Mr. Montagu who visited Madras, on behalf of the Crown in 1917, he complained against the British officials that they "voted themselves exorbitant salaries and large allowances; that they refuse us education; they sap up of our wealth; they impose crushing taxes without our consent; cast thousands of our people into prisons for uttering patriotic sentiments—prisons so filthy that often the inmates die from loathsome diseases" (*Ibid.*, p. 104).

The intensity of the political commitment can also be guaged from the fact that despite having been a career-judge and thus an automatic supporter of the *rule of law*, he is on record having written to the President Wilson of the USA in 1917, persuading him to interfere with the British government to concede Home Rule to India.

The inequitous character of the British rule and several discriminatory acts passed under it came for a severe critcism at the hands of several of these Indian judges, obviously when they were no longer in service. Illustratively, Badruddin Tayyabji, who played an extremely active role in public life and was also elected president of the Indian National Congress in 1887, launched a scathing tirade on some inequitous British laws. For example, addressing a public meeting in April 1883, he spoke on the Ilbert Bill Controversy as follows :

> "Further, gentlemen, what can be greater injustice to the whole Indian community than to declare even the ablest of our native magistrates and judges, no matter what their qualifications may be, as an inferior order of men, incapable of rising to that height of judicial excellence which is supposed to be necessary to try cases against Europeans ? Gentlemen, I venture to think that the present state of the law is not only unjust, but it is insulting to us (Cheers). It is insulting to us because it draws an invidious distinction between the European and the native members of the same Covenanted Civil Service. It is insulting to us because it exalts the European British subjects into such superior beings as to declare that even the highest of our judicial officers shall be incapable of imprisoning him a single day of fining him a single rupee; and it is insulting to us because it degrades our own countrymen to such a depth to declare in the very next breath that the same incompetent and unfit magistrates and judges, who are incapable of trying even the most trivial case of assault against an Englishman, are yet fit and competent to try millions of our own coutrymen for the gravest charges and even to condemn them to death ? (Loud and prolonged cheers.) Gentlemen, the height of absurdity could go no further, and yet forsooth these are the arguments ostensibly put forward

for the purpose of defeating this just, generous, and above all extremely moderate and cautious measure."

Not only that some inequitous laws formed by the British came in for severe criticism at the hands of these judges, but they also derived the lopsided perspective of the British on the Indian *nature*, *personality* and *temperament* with which they often buttressed their administrative acumen. For example, the Right Hon. Syed Amir Ali who served as a judge of the Calcutta High Court,

> —ridiculed the British conception of India as an easy-going country, run on fixed, generally unalterable lines—"the land of pageants and the home of durbars—the bulk of whose people untouched by the changes in the conception of the thinking classes occasioned by the contact of two civilizations—one old and stationary, the other young, active and utilitarian, bow down before official as an *avatar* of progress and prosperity".[14]

Some others like Sir C. Sankar Nair, were not only critical of the British for various inequities heaped upon Indians, but also understood the dynamics of their trained incapacity which prevented them from comprehending the Indian problems in a sensitive manner. Delivering Presidential address to the Congress in 1897, he said :

> An Englishman in India is in a strange world; with his energy, strong will, and ideas of freedom, he fails to understand and perhaps despises a nation given up to metaphysical dreams which does not regard material prosperity as the great object of life. In other parts of the world under European sway in Africa and America, an alliance with a European is eagerly sought while in India, where also he is master, he is regarded by the castes as impure, whose touch is pollution. With such differences in thought and feeling, no wonder that ordinary Englishmen ignore the people entirely and do not try to understand them. Hence their limited comprehension. Not knowing the native mind, they exaggerate the importance of

14. *Ibid.*, p. 234.

trifles which only ruffle the surface of native feeling and attribute to certain events a significance which, however justifiable in England, do not even deserve a passing notice in India.

2. Judges and Polity : Contemporary Context

The distinctive nature of relationship between the judges and the polity needs to be appreciated, in the post independence context. The Judges now serve an indigenous polity of which they themselves are a part, as against the Indian judges of the pre-independence era who served a political administration which was basically exogenous to the society in which they lived and which they ruled through dispensing justice. This difference is very significant because the institutional boundary separating judiciary from the political administration was well marked in the earlier historical situation but is relatively blurred in the contemporary situation. Theoretically, in the modern situation, both judges and political administrators being anchored in the same socio-cultural matrix, are bound to exercise a relatively closer impact upon each other. The politicians by manoeuvring the administrative system of rules and laws governing the judges would, therefore, try to achieve certain measure of control or constraint over the judges and thus imperil the strict compliance of professional objectivity; the judges at least some, if not all, would try to achieve and further their career-interests by placating and thus in the process, partially compromise their professional objectivity. An overview of the contemporary judicial scene corroborates these theoretical projections and surmises. No sociological researches have yet been undertaken in this area; hence whatever materials, informations, are available in the news-media or in the professional reports have been used here to substantiate the preceding argument.

First of all, all governments in the country since independence of 1947, have been using the formally available rules and procedures to influence judicial appointments. As evidenced from the controversy raging over governments' prerogative in transferring and promoting high court judges,[15] the appointments and transfers of judges have been influenced. The start was made in the well known case of supersession of three Supreme Court Judges and the consequent appointment of A. N. Ray as Chief Justice of India in 1973. The said appointment drew wild uproar from the lawyers, judges and politicians, but the Government even though disregarding the time-honoured convention of appointing the senior-most judge as the Chief Justice of the Supreme Court of India,[16] was, 'legitimately' using the prerogative available to it within the law. The fact that political pressure is brought to bear upon the judicial appointments has been emphasized by judges as well as some other keen observers of the legal scene such as the law-specialists and law-journalists on petitions pending before Supreme Court while challenging the implementation of the policy of transferring judges and appointing Chief Justices of High Courts from "other" states. A couple of years ago, a three-bench judge told the Union Government that it could hot "pick and choose" judges at its sweet will. All judges (D.A. Desai; A.P. Sen; V.D. Tulzapurkar) severely castigated the Union Government for having influenced the appointments of judges in the High Courts of Madhya Pradesh, Kerala, Rajasthan and Gujarat. As reported in a national daily.[17]

> "The most severe remarks came from Justice A. P. Sen, who declared that in the Rajasthan High Court, the Union Government's own policy of appointing the senior-most judges of that court had been violated and a senior judge had been taken as a Chief justice to Sikkim on purely political grounds. In

---

15. Since the famous case S. P. Gupta *v.* Union of India, 1981, Supp. SCC 87.

16. The relevant Act. 124 (2) of the Constitution of India, reads as follows :—

"Every judge of the Supreme Court shall be appointed by the President by warrant under his hand and seal after consultation with such of the judges of the Supreme Court and of the High Courts in the states as the President may deem necessary for the purpose and shall hold office until he attains the age of sixty five years."

17. The Hindustan Times, New Delhi, 27-4-1985.

the Madhya Pradesh High Court, Former Chief Justice G. P. Singh had blocked the list of 10 judges sought to be appointed *en bloc* on the ground that they were not fit to be appointed. Hence the next person in that court after the retirement of Mr. Singh was kept as the acting Chief Justice so that he clears all the 10 names recommended for appointment. Justice Sen continued that these names consisted of lawyers who had 'never appeared' in the High Court. The acting Chief Justice elected the list held back by his predecessor".[18]

In an interview given immediately after his retirement as Chief Justice of India, Mr. Chandrachud boldly asserted that,

> "Appointments which I opposed, were not made, names were recommended, names were strongly pressed, when I did not agree, those names were dropped."

Apart from the judges making such disclosures of political interference in the appointment of judges even,

> The famous 14th Report of the Law Commission submitted on September 26, 1958 described the malaise with a candour worthy of that body at its best. It "regretted" that there existed. "The general impression that now and again executive influence exerted from the highest quarters has been responsible for some appointments to the (Supreme Court) Bench"[19]

It is only against this enormous procedural and *de facto* power which the government can and does exercise over the judges via their transfers, appointments and promotions that strong fears expressed by some judges—both regarding government's high handedness and regarding surrender by some judges of their integrity and independence, can be understood and appreciated. Even some of the sitting Supreme Court Judges have expressed their anxieties at the growing sycophancy among the judges towards the

---

18. A. G. Noorani, "Crisis of Judiciary", *The Indian Express*, New Delhi, 30-4-1986.
19. *Ibid.*

government. Note for example Justice V. D. Tulzapurkar's anxiety :

> "The greatest enemy of a strong and independent judiciary would be the sycophant element within it—I mean Judges whose pre-dispositions and value systems keep on changing every time the ruling party changes........."[20]

Another instance of veiled sycophany given by Justice Tulzapurkar in the speech under mention is in the form of questionnaire issued by the Chairman of the Tenth Law Commission, Justice K. K. Mathew. He alludes to the following two questions inserted in the questionnaire, circulated by the Law Commission for seeking opinions on what should be done to improve the system of justice :

1. "Should the Supreme Court be replaced by a Constitutional Court dealing exclusively with Constitutional matters ?
2. Are you in favour of the establishment of a Court of Appeal as the final arbiter of disputes of Law (other than Constitutional Law) leaving the Supreme Court to concentrate on only Constitutional issues."

Tulzapurkar alleges in his speech that these questions are in no way related to the main objective of the Commission *i.e.* "to embark upon a study of the problem of evolving a methodology of speedier disposal of matters coming before the Supreme Court and High Courts", and are thus needless. Further, these questions reflect Justice Mathew's personal opinions and are intended to help the government overcome hurdles faced by it as a result of judgement on *Kesvanand Bharati's* case which prohibits it from interfering with the *basic structure* of the Constitution. (Kesvananda Bharati *v.* State of Kerala, 1973 AIR 1461 S.C.)

So severe is the pressure exercised by government's control over the careers and destinies of the judges that some of

20. V. D. Tulzapurkar : "Judiciary attacks and Survival", speech delivered at Pune on 29-10-1982, under the auspices of the Symbiosis Society, published in AIR Journal.

them are virtually reduced to the level of "hangers on" or minions of the politicians. Following is a picturesque description of various High Court Chief Justices converging on Delhi on the eve of Chief Justices Conference not so much for a professional or intellectual exchange, but for collecting some vital information to guide their careers :

> "Three kinds of Chief Justices of High Courts, which constitute the middle of the Indian judicial spine, came for the Chief Justice Conference on August 29, 30 and then for the Conference of Chief Justice, Chief Ministers and Law Ministers of the States on August 31, and September 1, 1985. There were those amongst the Chief Justices who knew and disliked the states they were proposed to be transferred to from their existing posts. There were others who wanted to find out the precise information concerning their future posting as part of the Union Government's policy (reiterated by the Prime Minister), of transferring Chief Justice to High Courts outside their home states. Several of them wanted to know their precise chances for elevation to the Supreme Court, since by practice the position of the Chief Justice of the High Court has become a stepping-stone to the Supreme Court. All these three categories of Chief Justices minus the few who still retain a heart's disdain for such manoeuvres landed in the capital a few days ago before August 29, to lobby for their respective roles through the channels of minister and other."[21]

Government seems to be using its prerogatives *vis-a-vis* the judges comprehensively to achieve its ends, to lessen its administrative burdens and sometimes to deflate the popular protest in the country. Look at the recent list of commissions constituted by the Government of India. As it can be appreciated all of these are concerned with the traumatic developments ensuing from

21. Krishan Mahajan, "C. Js : *Delhi Chalo*" under LEGAL PERSPECTIVES, in the *Hindustan Times*, New Delhi, 9-9-1985.

Mrs. Gandhi's assassination in October, 1984, and involved the appointment of various Supreme Court Judges—

Justice M. P. Thakkar (sitting)	Indira Gandhi Assassination case
Justice R. N. Mishra (sitting)	Delhi Sikh riots of 1984 following Mrs. Gandhi's Assassination
Justice V. B. Eradi (sitting)	Ravi Beas Commission dealing with the contentious issue of distribution of the water of Ravi & Beas between Punjab & Haryana
Justice K. K. Mathew (retired)	Boundary Dispute between Punjab & Haryana
E. S. Venkataramiah (sitting)	Exchange of territories between Punjab & Haryana
Justice D. A. Desai (retired)	Identification of areas to be transferred from Punjab & Haryana in lieu of transfer of Chandigarh to Punjab towards implementation of "Punjab Accord" signed between Prime Minister Rajiv Gandhi and the Akali leader Late H. S. Longowal.

Apart from the fact that such a step may also provide a cushion to the government of the day against growing public protest on several disputed issues, the appointments of the sitting judges on various "honorific" commissions could also mean "political" investments in these judges to be realized subsequently. But a dysfunction of all this overt and covert exchange of favours is bound to slow down the pace of justice at the apex courts in the country.

JUDICIARY'S ACTIVISM AND THE DEPARTURE FROM 'STATUS QUO'

Despite this inter-penetration of the judiciary and the polity, judicial activism has been a distinct institutional product of the highest judiciary during the past 5-6 years or so. Through this growing orientation, it has been making a distinctive contribution to the polity, unthought of earlier and altogether beyond the wildest idealism of pre-independence judiciary. Some judges in the Supreme Court and more particularly its reigning Chief Justice, Mr. Bhagwati, have been advocating a much more active role of the law as against the classical brand of justice along the lines of *locus standi.* On petitions filed by lawyers, journalists, social workers and even by some civil rights bodies such as PUCL, PUDR, on behalf of affected groups and classes of people who may have suffered neglect or injustice under the law,[22] mostly by way of denial of their fundamental rights, the Supreme Court has been going as far as appointing commissions of inquiry to collect fuller facts on certain public interest cases and then treating these reports as "evidences." Going still further, the court has also been appointing special officials to see that the orders passed by the court providing relief to the affected people were implemented. Note justice Bhagwati's own reporting :—

> "We, therefore, thought that it was necessary to evolve a methodology for securing enforcement of court orders in public interest litigation, and with this end in view, we started appointing monitoring agencies. In a case brought by a journalist for protection of women in police custody, the Supreme Court gave various directives and asked a woman judicial officer to visit the police lock-ups periodically and to report to the High Court whether the directives were being carried out."

Obviously, there is a juridical-philosophic assumption behind

22. P. N. Bhagwati, "Judicial Activism and Public Interest Litigation" *Address* delivered at the Columbia University School of Law, and published in *Columbia Journal of Transnational Law*, 23, 56, 1985, pp. 561-576.

this approach. On this, we reproduce below from one of the most outspoken critics of the existing legal system—Justice V. R. Krishna Iyer :

> "... Anglo-Saxon Law is transactional, highly individualistic concerned with an automistic justice incapable of responding to the claims and demands of collectively, and resistant to change. Such law was developed and has developed in an essentially individualistic society to deal with situations involving the private right/duty pattern. It cannot possibly meet the challenge raised by the new concerns for the social rights and collective claims of the under-privileged. What we, therefore, need to do is to fashion new strategies ... in fact evolve a new jurisprudence ... and find a new policy of collectivity as a back drop to our efforts."[23]

Or, a still more pungent comment from the same judge.

> "... we cannot allow the power of law to be cornered by the tycoons, the litigationists and the corporations which Lord Coke noticed centuries ago 'cannot commit treason, nor be outlawed, nor ex-communicated, for *they have no souls*'. These soul-less giants oppress the worker and the consumer, pollute air and water all environment and corrupt those in political power in all the branches so that a high tide of people's socio-legal action alone can call to order their outlaws'."[24]

Flamboyancy and stylistics has proverbially been a part of the judgements delivered by judges almost everywhere. Perhaps, the overadherence to the 'formal' and the 'factual' on their part has been automatically counterbalanced, as if, through a psychological compensation, by a virtuosity of flair and sermonising—encouraged all the more by the fact that on a case, judges have the last word to say and that they can say as many words as they like un-

23. V. R. Krishna Iyer, *Indian Justice*, Vedpal Law House, Indore, 1984, pp. 6-7.

24. *Ibid.*, p. 30.

inhabited by their audience or their peers on the bench. But then, in a certain social context, there is always a limit to a judge's 'creative' and off-beat outpourings, because all these have to be related to the facts of a case and the law or the laws that it is governed by. All the same, as a broad generalization, more of such 'creativity' can be expected from judges in fast-changing democracies than those working either in developed societies or in developing but non-democratic societies. The logic of this semi-theoretic statement is too explicit and simplistic to need any further elaboration and can be well illustrated through some of judgements issued by the Supreme Court of India in the recent years. All these would indeed merit a separate and a detailed study, but for the present, just one sample.

In petition *Nakara* v. *Union of India,*[25] heard by 5-judge bench, the simple case of pension rules—wherein the authorities intended to confine the benefit of a liberalising notification to employees retiring only after that notification became effective, was held as violative of Art. 14, which guarantees fundamental right of equality before the law. Instead, the Court ruled that employees retiring both before and after the said notification of March-Sept. 1979, constituted one composite category and should be entitled to receive the benefits under the said revision. While reacting to the government counsel's plea that constituting *one* out of *two* sub-categories was not justified and without any precedent, justice D. A. Desai, who delivered the judgement averred as follows :—

> "The last submission, the absence of precedent need not deter us for a moment. Every new norm of socio-economic justice, every new measure of social justice commenced for the first time at some point of history. If at that time it is rejected as being without a precedent, the law as an instrument of social engineering would have long since been dead and no tears would have been shed. To be pragmatic is not to be unconstitutional. In its onward march law as an institution ushers in socio-economic justice. In fact, social security in old age commended itself in earlier stages as a moral concept but in

25. Supreme Court Cases, 1985, Vol. I, pp. 304-345.

course of time it acquired legal connotation. The rules of natural justice owed their origin to ethical and moral code. Is there any doubt that they become the integral and inseparable parts of rule of law of which any civilised society is proud? Can anyone be bold enough to assert that ethics and morality are outside the field of legal formulations? Socio-economic justice stems from the concept of social morality coupled with abhorrence for economic exploitation. And the advancing society converts in course of time moral or ethical code into enforceable legal formulations. Over-emphasis on precedent furnishes an insurmountable road-block to the onward march towards promised millennium. An overdose of precedents is the bane of our system which is slowly getting stagnant, stratified and atrophied. Therefore, absence of a precedent on this point need not deter us at all. We are all the more happy for the chance of scribbling on a clean slate."

Further,

"If it appears to be undisputable, as it does to us that the pensioners for the purpose of pension benefit from a class, would its upward revision permit a homogeneous class to be divided by arbitrarily fixing an eligibility criteria unrelated to purpose of revision, and would such classification be founded on some rational principle? The classification has to be based, as is well settled, on some rational principle and the rational principle must have nexus to the objects sought to be achieved. We have set out the object underlying the payment of pension. If the state considered it necessary to liberalise the pension scheme, we find no rational principle behind it for granting these benefits only to those retired subsequent to that date simultaneously denying the same to those who retired prior to that date. If the liberalisation was considered necessary for augmenting social security in old age to government servants then those who retired earlier cannot be worse off than those who retire later. Therefore, this division which classified pensioners into two classes is not based on any rational principle and if the rational principle is the one of dividing pensioners with a view to giving something more to persons otherwise equally placed, it would be discriminatory." (*Ibid.*)

The 'social' argument employed in the above judgement is indeed delectable, and seems an even blend of Benjamin Cardozo's *sociological* reasoning and the Jacobites' swearing by the goddess of Reason, in the eighteenth century revolutionary France. But the whole question of sociological relevance *i.e.* how many of the total judgements given by Supreme Court of India are likely to be characterized by this penchant for *humanistic* departure, and what weight this *departure* is, going to carry among the rest of the 'brother judges ?' An appropriate answer to this question would enable us to relate judiciary to the future of Indian polity.

THE SUMMING UP

A rather fragmented and disjointed discussion of the evolving relationship between the legal profession and the Indian polity over the past two hundred years or so brings out several interesting features. First of all, there is a definitive break in this relationship from independence (1947) onwards. The barest minimum consideration worthy of relevance is that the political response of the profession in the pre-independence context was essentially anti-systemic, one way or the other, since the polity was perceived essentially extraneous to the indigenous social reality. This anti-polity stance, however, in this historical setting is nearly exclusive to practising lawyers. The reasons for this lie partly in that the judges are internal to the politico-legal system the way lawyers are not, and have thus an automatic and 'professional' directionality in its perpetuation. That is, functionally as well as consequentially, judges work more for the continuation and preservation of the system than the lawyers who are more interested in extractions from the legal system, to be used in the interest of their clients. That is why, the critique of the system by the pre-independence judges rarely goes beyond the humanistic appraisal and evaluation of its processes and functioning. As against this, the lawyers are seen taking clearly anti-systemic position for the simple reason that they are liberated from custodial constraints which produce natural loyalty to the legal system among the judges.

The scenario as it opened after independence ushered lawyers headlong into the task of constitution-making, which is indeed a momentous document inhering both the Gandhian values of participative administration through institutions like panchayati raj etc. as well as values of secularism, egalitarianism, equal access to justice etc. Lawyers continue to dominate even now in both the houses of national legislature and handle important ministerial portfolios. But, that is where the collective concern on the part of practising profession, for the institution-making seems to have climaxed and ended simultaneously. But the manner and motive of political involvement is more atomised and individualistic, and seems bereft of any political or macro-societal concerns. Now, legal expertise among those who are active in public life has almost become a *cash nexus*, tradeable with whatever political party lawyers are able to form a workable equation. This in a certain sense thus implies the nemesis of collective social concerns on the part of the Indian legal profession.

Another important dimension of the contemporary legal scene is the growth of judicial activism. Judges who earlier never went as far as holding in disrepute the contemporary polity or legal system are now growing strongly critical of such of their features as are incongruent with the letter and spirit of the constitution. Disregarding the traditional legal procedures such as those of precedent or *locus standi* on issues of larger public interest involving especially the poorer and the indigent classes of people, they are trying to provide quick relief to the under-privileged. Notable contributions have been rendered to this phenomenon also by certain public-spirited lawyers, legal journalists of activist orientations as well as various civil liberties organizations. But this syndrome of legal activism as yet lacks some organized institutional form and, therefore, may be living a dicey 'existence', despite providing a progressive and egalitarian push to the state of things in society.

CHAPTER TWO

ELECTION OF THE BAR PRESIDENT

AT THE LAST bar elections in 1974, one Mr. Himmat Singh was elected President of the Gobindgarh District Court bar. This means the defeat of the sitting President Mr. Upender Nath Aggarwal, a *Bania* by caste. Mr. Himmat Singh, even though having a Sikh name and an outward expression of a Sikh—long hair and uncut beard, is a Brahmin by caste. He is reported to have carried with him the support of both the Brahmins as well as Sikh members of the bar in addition to the *en-block* support of the members of the Young Lawyers Association (YLA)—a body within the Gobindgarh Bar Association having forty odd members. Almost, all these youger members are mostly with less than ten years of standing at the bar. The outcome of the election is hailed as of dramatic significance and a trendsetter in many ways, nearly by all the groups and factions of the bar.

This is the first time ever that the bar elected a Sikh member as its president. This is true only to the extent that one recognizes Himmat Singh as a "Sikh" since he comes of a Brahmin caste even though he is completely identified as a Sikh by the bar members. None among the forty odd members of the bar who were questioned on the election differed with this version, one of them saying that his having been drawn from a Brahmin caste was peripheral and insignificant in view of the fact that he lived his life with and among Sikhs. His father had been a divinity teacher (a *gyani*) in a Sikh Missionary School at Gobindgarh and lived the life of Sikhs. He (Himmat Singh) himself is also reported to have had long-standing contacts with the Sikh politicians. It was reported that he had been the favourite of Sardar Partap Singh Kairon, the ex-Chief Minister of Punjab and had a flourishing practice during his time. He used to get most of his criminal briefs through his reported intimacy with the police and politicians and through his reported efficiency to 'get things done'. Ever since, Sardar Partap Singh Kairon died and Akalis captured power in the State, his practice flopped. 'This did not effect him and he continued to have a descent income of Rs. 3000 to 3500 per month. He seems to be satisfied with his practice. In addition, he devoted all the time he had at his disposal in cultivating contacts with the bar members. It was reported by some of the very intimate compaigners of Upendra Nath Aggarwal, that,

> ". . . . He (*i. e.* Himmat Singh) set his mind on winning the bar election right from the day that Aggarwal got elected last time. He stopped his political wandering and started spending most of his time with the bar members. He already had a straight and clear equation with seventy odd Sikh members of the bar, particularly with the 45 Jat members with whom he shared both a common culture and a background. Even though being a criminal practitioner himself, he would sit most of the time in the enclosure occupied by criminal lawyers, yet he tried as far as possible to reach all the Sikh members."

Himmat Singh made use of another two very significant factors in order to strengthen his support in the bar. These were: (1) Professional Jealousies, and (2) Jealousies of the younger *vis-a-vis* the senior members of the bar-articulated through the Young Lawyers' Association (YLA), a splinter association within the overall Gobindgarh District Bar Association. As some close associates of Himmat Singh divulged, he had picked up some lawyers who were professional rivals of Aggarwal andg were practising on the civil side. From these rivals of Mr. Aggarwal, he went down to their juniors or to their sons whom he used to his own advantage through a combination of comraderie, persuasion, bribery, drinks etc. As one Swaroop Singh, a young lawyer who compaigned for Himmat Singh stated :

> ". . . . .We had a hunch that the secretary of the Gobindgarh Bar Association—Mr. Rajinder Arora whose father was a

bitter rival of Mr. Aggarwal can be used to enhance the chances of our candidate. In the fortnight preceding the elections, we surreptitiously brought some new members from the adjacent *Tehsil* bars and also from the adjacent district bars, to be enrolled members at the Gobindgarh Bar Association. We took Rajinder into confidence so that he should not disclose this fact to the other side. . . . .We mustered about sixty such fresh members, all of whom were bound to support our candidate."

Hear, now the connecting narration from an intimate supporter of Mr. Aggarwal, one Mr. Agnihotri;

"Lalaji (Agarwal) had gone to Bombay on the marriage of his grand-daughter, from where he returned only on 19th Dec. Meanwhile Rajinder had been playing into the hands of Himmat Singh and his men and had been helping them in swelling the ranks of their supporters through enrolling new members from all over the district and even from outside. Lalaji told me on his return that he was not satisfied with the campaigning already done in connection with the forthcoming election and asked me to take stock of his electoral strength from the list of the bar membership. I looked into the bar register and was stunned to note that the other side had a clear edge over us on account of the surreptitious enrolment of sixty odd members from outside. . . .I asked Rajinder how it happened. He reported that everything was as per the rules and the Constitution of the Bar Association which governed the affairs of the Gobindgarh. It was perfectly correct in so far as the rules were concerned, but, then there is something like propriety with which a general secretary of the bar should behave. Even though there was no law against this enrolment, yet he should have informed the then President of the bar (Lalaji) of this development. That is what our side felt. I intimated the situation to Lalaji and he was very angry. He asked me on the twentieth of December to go all over Punjab and enrol such lawyers as the members as were sure to support his candidature. . . . .

> . . . I returned with about seventy five membership forms duly filled and reached the bar office in the courts at 3 P.M. . . That was the last day when new memberships could be entertained and the closing time as per our constitution was 4 P.M. I had to submit these forms to the General Secretary—Mr. Rajinder. I looked for him feverishly but he was nowhere to be seen. I spoke to his assistant in the bar room at 3.45 P.M. and wanted to know Rajinder's whereabouts. He said, he just did not know where he was and could not accept the forms on his own . . . . Finally, he appeared at about 4 P.M, I dashed for him and placed the new membership—applications with the subscription money before him. Just as he started scrutinising the forms as if by a pre-fixed stratagem, around fifteen lawyers most of them Jat Sikhs thronged me and started shouting 'time is up ! No new membership now. . ."

This really enraged Aggarwal and he had a stay filed in the local court through one of his supporters alleging mismanagement in the bar affairs and praying that the bar elections be stayed and not held on 22nd December. The Magistrate concerned was afraid to interfere in the affairs of the bar and immediately proceeded on leave. Meanwhile this move on the part of Aggarwal alienated him from a majority of the bar members since he had taken an internal dispute of the bar to a court of law. As was stylishly put by one fifty year old civil lawyer :

> "With this step, Aggarwal was seen blackening his face with his own hands."

The general secretary of the Bar, Rajinder was approached by some supporters of Himmat Singh with an application signed by other hundred members, that the general body meeting be called to consider the legal step taken by president of the bar. Meeting was called where the members demanded that the elections be held on 22nd December, as already fixed. There was a complete pandemonium as supporters from both the sides started shouting slogans. The president left the meeting in a huff saying "I adjourn the meeting". The members of the bar in general took a very serious view of it and wanted the meeting to continue till a satisfactory decision was arrived at. One Mr. Pritam Singh, a sixty year old Sikh criminal lawyer was elected president for the duration of the meeting. It was decided that the elections be held on 22nd December as already scheduled. Himmat Singh had all his supporters ready to vote, whereas many of Aggarwal's supporters bycotted the election as a protest against the 'high-handed conduct' of the general body meeting by the supporters of Himmat Singh. Elections were held and Himmat Singh won with a heavy margin of 194/17.

The Young Lawyer Association is within the Gobindgarh Bar Association and is only two years old. Its forty-odd members fall within the age-bracket of 25-37 years and have a maximum of 12 years of experience at the Gobindgarh Bar. One Mr. Nirmal Singh, an enthusiastic member of the YLA, reported as follows :

> ". . . Our organization came into being with a view to safeguard the interests of the younger members who get next to no help from the elder members of the bar. As everyone knows, more than eighty per cent of the business at the district courts is monopolized by about ten per cent of the bar members and the remaining ninety per cent of bar members compete among themselves for merely ten per cent of the business. . . .The position is all the worse in the case of the youngsters whom even the bench (i.e. Judges) refuses to give any consideration, by way postponements etc. So often we need to get some help or guidance from the senior members of the bar. An experience which me and my colleague had in this regard is really heart-rending. Once, two of us were engaged in a case which was a little too complicated for us. We decided to call on one of our senior colleagues practising on the civil side. When we reached his place, he was busy with some clients. We had to wait for nearly one hour in the waiting room, after which he came out and walked away saying that 'I do not have any time to spare'. . . "

Himmat Singh knew this state of frustration of the young

lawyers and had been very nice to them for the last one year, cultivating half a dozen close personal associations among them—especially the Sikh members of Young Lawyers Association. He had been throwing frequent drink parties to these youngsters long time before the elections took place. He requested some of these youngsters to go on a membership-campaign to the nearby Tehsil and district courts—especially during the month preceding the elections. They worked for him and got him many supporters from outside Gobindgarh. Once again, these youngsters were the very lawyers who stood in the way of Rajinder accepting the membership-forms which Agnihotri, one of Aggarwal's supporters, had brought with him from the election tour, immediately before the election took place.

As verified from the records, eighty per cent (80 per cent) of the newly recruited members who voted for Himmat Singh were drawn from Jat Sikhs and were obtained by Himmat Singh mostly through his personal contacts with the young Jat Sikh members of YLA, who had worked and campaigned for him all through. As extensive interviews with the YLA and the other members of the general bar revealed, before the elections took place and Himmat Singh was elected president, he was in no position to help anybody or even to hold any promise of professional help to anybody, since he had no professional practice worth the name, nor did he have any client—network which he could put at the disposal of anyone for professional help and support. He did not even carry the image of a knowledgeable lawyer so as to promise any free consultation to anybody. The point we were making is that none of those who campaigned for Himmat Singh and much hope of deriving any professional benefit from later on. The Jat lawyers, especially those who were members of the YLA, seemed to have seen in this a historic defeat of the urban Bania and a victory for Jats Following expression of a member of YLA :

> "....It is very clear that the urban Sikhs have to fight alongside us in order to prevent victory of the Bania classes. Even though Jats constitute around one third of the district court bar, they get only about ten per cent of the total

business done there. In criminal practice, only a couple of lawyers from our community have a good standing at the bar. But in civil practice, we have no representation whatsoever. Even 'Revenue' cases which originate in the villages are monopolized by the urban Hindus. None among the 'first three choices' practising on this side happens to be a Sikh—what to say of a Jat. In terms of money these urban Hindus grab among themselves nothing short of 80 per cent of the total business. And the only people blocking our entry into this area are the urban Hindus, especially the Banias. . . The election gave us opportunity of at least putting one of us in a leading position. This was a scarce opportunity and none among us wanted to miss it. Finally, we are happy that Himmat Singh is elected President."

The entire preceding discussion leads to the inference that the discontent of Jat lawyers, especially the younger ones was channelised through the opportunity provided by the candidature of Himmat Singh, and the cohesiveness exhibited by them was only a collective expression of their desire to occupy a meaningful economic-professional space at the courts. The same expression of discontent was noticed at *Shergarh Tehsil** bar. The Jats who constituted only 46 per cent of the total Shergarh bar were consolidating their political forces. One forty-two years old Jat Sikh practising here remarked :

> "Most of the business and industry of the town is in the hands of the Hindus. Since the Jats during their visits to the tehsil headquarter make most of their purchases such as fertilizers, provisions, cloth, etc. at the shops of Hindu shopkeepers, the lawyers connected or related with these shopkeepers do get many clients through these links. Thus, such of the Revenue business also comes to these lawyers."

Another conspicuous advantage which some of the Hindu lawyers of Shergarh seem to have over their Jat sikh counterparts

*One of the four constituting *tehsil* courts of the Gobindgarh District co urts.

is that through their membership in the Shergarh Municipal Committee, they seem to attract more clientele than they would otherwise do. According to one Hindu Khatri who is member of the municipal committee :

> "... In attracting clientele, it does matter what your social position is. I am doing criminal practice and I know from my experience that among reasons which send a client to me, not the least important is that I am a municipal commissioner and should, therefore, be knowing the magistracy and the local police. It does fill a client with a feeling of assurance while he decides to come and, without being hypocritical, I must tell you that this belief on the part of the clients is not unfounded ... My father had been a president of the committee and now I have been its member for quite sometime. This has definitely given our family a fair amount of prestige in the local society. Both the police high-ups as well as some members of judiciary feel nice about cultivating friendship with me. Now I do not have to go out of the way to create an impression on them, all of them know me too well. Moreover, my membership of the local Rotary club is also an important factor. This advantage which a person like me has, is not enjoyed by any of the Jat members of the bar, simply because they do not belong to the town."

The fact that there is cleavage between the Jats and non-Jats at Shergarh Tehsil bar was also reported by the record-keeper of the Bar Association, a Brahmin boy who comes from a local business family.

> "... The Jat members of the bar resent that they are not able to get a good share of the business available at the Shergarh court. As I have been going into legal practice here because of increased literacy among Jats. But, they have not so far posed any competition for the local Hindu lawyers since they cannot cut out an impressive image even among the Jat brothers who think [that a "Shehiri Bau" (*i.e.* a city based

lawyer) is more learned and can talk better before the magistrate than a Jat lawyer. . . ."

In the overall sense even though majority of the lawyers comprised of Sikhs, local Hindu lawyers have been able to isolate Jat sikhs from the urban non-Jats and win the support of the latter as against the former. As a result of this, both the general secretary and the president of the Shergarh bar are drawn from urban-based Hindu lawyers.

CHAPTER THREE

PROFESSIONAL COGNITION AND PROFESSIONAL DECEPTION–A SOCIOLOGICAL PROJECTION OF LAWYERS' ROLE IN LEGAL AID PLAN

I. BACKGROUND

THE TWIN objective of our national planning—as of the entire Third World, is to remove poverty and sharp inequalities and disparities among various sections of population. This may be seen as the logical extension of our very commitment to the idea of a *democratic* polity enshrined both in constitution as well as in various other documents of state policy and planning.[1] The toning down of sharp economic disparities and the removal of poverty are seen as mutual adjuncts, since the former is supposed to generate circumstances and conditions leading to the latter *i.e.* weakening the very basis of poverty in society.[2] This line of

1. Even though this linkage between development and reduction of sharp economic inequalities is too manifest in our national planning, to require any illustration from one document or the other, yet the following quote from the Second Five Year Plan, conveys the point clearly enough :

"The problem before under-developed countries embarking upon development at this late state is to so plan the alignment of productive resources and of class relationships as to combine development with reduction in economic and social inequality : the process and pattern of development has not so far been attempted on any significant scale under democratic conditions. There are no historical parallels or plans of action which could be regarded as providing an answer to this special problem facing underdeveloped countries." (Government of India, *Planning Commission, The First Five Year Plan–A draft outline*, New Delhi, 1951, p. 11).

2. This line of reasoning to view these two in their mutual relationship, is stylized by Gunnar Myrdal as "egalitarian ideals" of the equalization ideology", which manifestly is applicable to the rest of South Asia. See his Asian Drama, Vol. II, Allen Lane, The Penguin Press, London, 1968, pp. 743-45.

reasoning is quite clear in our national planning though by itself it can achieve precious little unless converted into an operational strategy. The demand and supply-based market economy that we have militates against the translation of this thinking into actual reality. First of all, we cannot, within the existing political and economic framewark, deprive the affluent members of society of their material means and resources and thus reduce the gap between "haves" and "have-nots". Secondly, through no *defensible* law, 'flat' or commandment of the state can we prevent them from multiplying their assets through a vast variety of 'legitimate' investments and reinvestments, thus widening the existing distance between the rich and the poor. All this leads upto one obvious deduction that the reduction of gap between the "haves" and "have-nots" requires some radical policy-innovations, tending to improvise the existing institutional structures for the immediate relief and benefit of the poor, pending the long term consequences of certain "fundamental" changes in the policy.

One such institutional innovation is sought to be attempted through the proposed legal aid programme, whereby the poor and the indigent are provided benefit of "free" legal consultation and representation in a court of law.[3] The objective inherent in this programme is to close the gap between *structural poverty* and the capacity to invoke law in defence of one's claims and rights. The implication of this programme is that, left to their own resources, the poor cannot obtain such proceeds or pay-offs from the existing legal system which is a more effective tool in the hands of the rich which they use for the defence and furtherance of their interests rather than in the hands of the poor and indigent. This, indeed, is a loud commentary on the retrogressive and inegalitarian character of our legal system which is expressly tilted towards the rich as against the poor. Since the legal system is a part and parcel of

---

3. Several other policy measures already taken or proposed to be taken by the Indian Government, such as free or subsidized access to medical facilities or to education, interest-free or low-interest loans etc. for the benefit of the poor and indigent belong to the same genre of institutional facilities or improvisations. They are all meant to moderate immediately the existential severities of poverty.

the overall systemic reality, the entire framework of democracy with all its institutional ramifications becomes suspect.

The *modus operandi* of providing legal aid is to take away the burden of lawyer's fee from the shoulders of the poor client. The same is now proposed to be paid either by the state or by any voluntary agency or organization; or, even the lawyers themselves may waive off their professional *fees* and render *free* legal assistance to indigent and resourceless clients. The inference implicit in this proposed modality is that *lawyer's fee* constitutes the heaviest charge on a poor client, so that once it is taken care of, nothing separates him from justice.[4]

Our contention here is that the assumption underlying this sanguine optimism is too blatant and fundamental and cannot be accepted casually. It must be asked squarely : firstly, whether it is at all possible to provide lawyer's fee on behalf of all indigent clients, and secondly; even if this is done, is it possible to obtain 'genuine' assistance from the lawyer *i.e.* the one which he would have provided in case the client himself had the capacity to make this payment ? In the subsequent sections of this paper, we shall try to seek answers to several such questions related to this assumption and infer whether or not *free legal aid* as an antidote to poverty of the masses is a viable proposition and can serve any significant ends. If not what are the reasons which are likely to jeopardize the success of this mechanism ?

We shall conduct this examination at two levels : at the level of professional relations or the relations between the lawyers and their clients, and at the level of professional cognitions *i.e.* the way lawyers relate themselves and their profession to the overarching socio-political and cultural reality. These two together, our heuristic assumption is, would provide the substantive poten-

4. Of the various cost-components that go into the total litigation cost on a case, another important component besides the lawyer's fee is the court fee required to be paid by each litigant. As of now, the court if it so chooses, can waive off this charge under the *forma pauperis*. But, all the same, the court fee, required to be paid especially by the poor claimants is insignificant as compared to the lawyer's fee. Hence, the major emphasis in the proposed legal aid programme is on the assistance to the indigent to pay the counsel's fee.

tial for the success or failure of the proposed plan. We must also state another heuristic assumption adopted for the purpose of this study. The term *legal professional*, examined by us in this chapter extends both to the lawyers and judges. We may advance two pragmatic justifications for this conceptual improvisation. First, both lawyers and judges are qualified lawyers. Second, quite a significant component of judiciary—especially the higher judiciary is built up from amongst the practising lawyers. As a result, their cognitive perspectives are bound to be closely correspondent to each other. This may also be so on account of another structural reason, *viz*. both lawyers and judges are insiders to the legal system inasmuch as their professional products in the form of court-judgements as well as lawyers' expertise matter crucially for the interests of the clients who are *outsiders* to this system. Still further, both lawyers and judges discharge their professional function using the same *abstract body of legal knowledge*. This similarity of structural position is likely to bring about a broad correspondence of cognitive perspectives. Hence this conceptual improvisation :

The discussion which follows will be arranged under two sections : Structure of Professional Relations and, Structure of Professional Cognitions, which is in keeping with the arrangement in the preceding.

II. STRUCTURE OF PROFESSIONAL RELATIONS

It is not without reason that the major emphasis of the entire legal aid programme is on ensuring the availability of lawyers' professional expertise for the benefit of the indigent clients. The latter cannot deal with the former from any position of strength because of their sheer dependence upon the former's professional skills and expertise. This dependence is of a comprehensive nature. Not only that knowledge and technicalities of law are shrouded in mystery for the unwary clients, but even the routine and elementary procedures such as those required for filing case-papers in a court of law, or those required for obtaining copies of court judgement are beyond their comprehension. All these further add to the client's helplessness by a constant display of nervous tension before their counsels who therefore, spare no efforts in exploiting this vulnerability of theirs. As inferred by author from his field researches, the anxiety experienced by clients also gets accentuated by a perceived cultural lag between themselves and their counsels.[5] All this *mystifies* law in the perspective of clients and leads to a pontification of lawyers in their estimation.[6] The lawyer is fully aware of this asymmetry and inequity of relationship and thus spares no opportunity of converting this awareness into pecuniary advantage.

There are several manifestations of this professional exploitation already well known to public and to the professional world to require any detailed enumeration. All the same, all these may be collectively recognized as acts of *unprofessionality*[6(i)] in that they run counter to what the lawyers themselves recognize should be observed by them *professionally*. For example against the well-accepted professional norms of 'charging fee only once' for a case, most of the lawyers are known to be making all varieties of extortions from their clients on some pretext or the other. It is also a well known fact that lawyers always try to 'develop' one case—initially assigned, into several cases and charge separate fees for all such cases.[7] Both these practices are "unprofessional" not only in the sense that they constitute a departure from any theoretical model of *professionality*, but in their being regarded as "unprofessional" by the professionals themselves. In a case study carried out by the author and cited in the preceding, district court lawyers viewed these practices as "unprofessional", but also accepted that they were wide-spread in the profession.

5. J. S. Gandhi, *Lawyers and Touts : A Study in the Sociology of Legal Profession*, Hindustan Publishing Corporation, New Delhi, 1982.

6. This point has a special relevance in the context of Indian legal reality, where most of the litigants having been drawn from rural areas, are still further distantiated from their counsels than their Western counterparts. Consequently the veil of mystery thickens all the more between the clients and their lawyers, making them all the more vulnerable to professional exploitation.

6(i) A copious evidence on the lawyer's malpractices also occurs in another worthy study. K. L. Sharma: *Sociology of Law and Legal Profession*, Rawat, Jaipur, 1982.

7. Interestingly enough, the skill to spin one case into many is viewed among the lawyers themselves as a measure of one's professional maturity and efficiency. So, the intra-professional perception of this practice promotes it all the more instead of discouraging it through censure.

The above two illustrations are intended only to sample the professional reality, since there is an endless variety of such and still subtler varieties of professional exploitation and extortions—all of which highlight the uniquely powerful position that a lawyer occupies *vis-a-vis* his client.

The central assumption underlying the whole legal aid programme is that once the fee to the lawyer is paid on behalf of the indigent client by some outside agency, he will acquire automatic access to the professional expertise of a lawyer and consequently to justice. But, such an argument seems tenable only if it can be assumed that after fee is paid for a client, he would no more be exploitable at the hands of the lawyer, or that, the latter will have no propensity to exploit him, will seek no other 'remuneration' or consideration through any of the various devious means open to him. But such an expectation would be in violent departure from the reality and structure of professional relations as actually in existence, in which lawyer-professional is supreme and brooks no delay or hesitation in exploiting his client. What are then the consequences most likely to follow when a certain agency such as a voluntary organization or even the state pays fee on behalf of an indigent client to a lawyer who enjoys immense exploitative power *vis-a-vis* his client ?

First and the foremost consequence would be that since the lawyer would be charging fee openly and explicitly under a programme with pronounced "welfare" connotations about it, he is likely to charge less than the *total accretion* which he would otherwise collect from a client on his own, as a result of several 'professional' improvisations. He would, therefore, naturally try to resist the pressure to accept indigent's case if he can bag alternative business on his own. Or, on the event of being compelled to accept a case through pressures of professional adversity or persuasion, he would use several of the available ways and means for extorting "additional" doses of money from his client. In case, the latter refuses to oblige him with extra 'fee' or 'fees', the lawyer concerned is more likely to render "spurious" and "surfacial" professional assistance rather than the "genuine" one. This is likely to be so because there is no check of whatsoever type—professional, statutory or otherwise, that is likely to operate against it and defend the interests of the client. As a net result of this 'forced' professional morality on the lawyers, the clients' interests would fall into a still greater jeopardy. The crux of the above discussion, therefore, is that, even the best-intended legal aid programme is doomed to failure, on account of un-equal, or asymmetrical relationship in which the lawyers have the power to exploit the helpless clients. There is no *revolution* of professional attitudes or orientations, yet on record, in the Indian society, which is likely to turn these professional opportunists into willing protectors of the poor and indigent. As a result, even if they are "coerced" into charging less or-not-at-all from their clients, they still have so many methods and mechanisms in their repertory for making the clients succumb to any of the several exactions they are capable of imposing on them. Or, alternatively, the "service" or "aid" rendered would be more "spurious" than "genuine", more "surfacial" than "substantive", of no use to the poor clients at all, in their struggle against the rich and well-to-do who are capable of managing and manipulating the legal system, both at the macro and micro levels.

Lack of Professional Norms

The solitary mechanism which can generate a genuine willingness among the lawyers for rendering professional assistance to the poor citizens, is in the form of appropriate guidelines and directives issued by professional bodies existing at various levels.[8] In

8. In fact, the capacity of professional bodies to control the behaviour of their constituent members is the crucial and determining mark of a "profession" as against a simple "occupation". As a result, if the members of a profession are no longer amenable to the code of professional norms and ethics evolved by their professional organizations, they cease to belong to a *profession*, which then degenerates to the level of an ordinary occupation, job or a sundry source of earning livelihood. The moment this happens, the said *profession* no longer remains entitled to various privileges such as that of *autonomy to manage its own affairs*, which it enjoys from society. This is the position taken in most of the literatures on Sociology of Professions, e.g. (1) A.M. Saunders and P.A. Wilson, *The Professions*, London, 1933; (2) W.J. Goode, "Encroachment, Charlatanism and the Emerging Professions", *American Sociological Review*, 25, December 1960; (3) B. Barber, "Some Problems in the Sociology of the Professions", *Daedalus*, 92, 4, 1963.

other words, Bar Councils, other professional organizations or associations can take initiative for creating or defining new professional norms to be observed by their member-lawyers, and these should have the net effect of revolutionising their orientation towards the poor and indigent clients. These norms should be so clearly defined and the professional bodies should use appropriate sanctions for their observance, through monitoring their compliance and implementation closely and regularly. As a result, a lawyer who outrightly refuses to be guided by these norms in his day-to-day professional conduct, should face the danger of professional ostracisation. It, in fact, calls for a revolution of professional ethos !

It is a sad commentary on these bodies that they constitute at present a very feeble sanction for their constituents, exercising no or negligible corrective control over the professional conduct or behaviour. Every now and then, all of them seem to voice their strong professional concerns over issues which pose direct or indirect threat to their professional-economic interests. However, there has yet to be a meeting or a conference organized voluntarily by these professional bodies, espousing the interests of the poor and indigent. As a counter to it, one recalls dozens of legal aid conferences and seminars held in the country during the last five years or so, as a sequel to some important policy-pronouncements by the Government of India, its law minister, etc. declaring state's commitment to back up any legal aid programme. It can be checked up from the records of these bodies both during the *Congress* as well as *Janata* regimes that the periods of silence on the legal-aid programmes, on the part of these professional bodies, corresponded precisely to periods of passivity on the part of governments of these times. Another indicator of the utter lack of professional concern for the client's indigency is a near-absence of censure of such lawyers as are engaged in professional improprieties towards their clients. In fact, the whole history or rather histories of various provincial Bar Councils during the last thirty odd years of independent India would hardly reveal even a handful of such cases pursued against the defaulting members with any permanent or temporary damage to their career or reputation. This is indeed a very serious lacunae which is bound to come in the way of effective implementation of the legal aid programme—a programme intended to neutralise, though partly, the existential deprivations of the Indian masses. The problem, it must be recapitulated here, is twofold : the inadequate sensitivity and urge of the professionals to apply their professional expertise to ease the poverty of the masses, and the feebleness of sanctions—persuasive or coercive, exercised by professional bodies on their members, to rectify several professional improprieties and to tone up their average professional morality.

III. STRUCTURE OF PROFESSIONAL COGNITIONS

Needless to say that a professional's behaviour would be determined by the nature of his professional and social perceptions. In other words, the way he maps the cognitive reality around himself, both professional and social, would constitute his propensity to promote or frustrate a programme such as the one under examination. The cognitions would also influence in a strong manner his orientation towards his clientele or the way he allows his relations with his clientele to be structured. The present section will consider the nature and structure of such professional cognitions.

Phenomenologically, it is very difficult to disengage "professional" cognitions from the total range of cognitions in the personality of lawyers, since all cognitions exist in mutual interrelationship and influence each other in a multiplicity of ways. However, notwithstanding the complexity of this problem we shall focus our attention on certain cognitions which for operational purposes, we have termed as "professional". These concern expressions and articulations made by lawyers in two *collective* contexts rather than as *individuals*. These are: (*i*) remarks, comments and speeches made by lawyers during a professional convention called with a view to take a formal position on the issue of independence of judiciary,[9] and, (*ii*) opinions, perceptions and

9. All India Convention of Lawyers on the Independence of Judiciary, New Delhi, on 11-12 August 1973 held at Vigyan Bhawan.

arguments of various lawyers as well as their professional bodies on the issue of providing legal aid to the poor.[10] These cognitions may also be regarded "professional" in another sense, that all these touch upon lawyers' perception of their own profession and the relationship it bears both with state and society.

The two sets of cognitions analysed here differ from each other in one important respect. The first belong to a convention held of lawyers and judges which could also be regarded as a collective professional response to a situation of *challenge* and *insecurity* in which the professional collectivity found itself consequent upon the appointment of Justice A. N. Ray as the Chief Justice of Supreme Court by the Government, superseding some other senior judges in 1973. This exercise of 'discretion' on the part of government was perceived as interference with the autonomy of judiciary, which alone is considered entitled to make such recommendations. The second set of cognitions constitute a voluntaristic response of the profession to the proposal to introduce a scheme of free professional assistance to the poor and indigent clients. As it will be seen, both these situations provided to the lawyers, opportunities for entering into much wider reflections than warranted by the limited nature of issues involved. As a result, their cognitions and reflections ranged from the *political set up in the country* and the *nature* of *Indian Constitution* to the *issues of judicial and professional autonomy*. We shall analyse these two sets of cognitions separately in the first instance, and then collate them to draw some general inferences.

(A) Convention

The occasion for the lawyers to reflect on the independence of judiciary was provided by the appointment of Justice A. N. Ray as the Chief Justice of the Supreme Court of India 1973 superseding certain other judges who were senior to him in tenure and service. All the

10. Law Commission of India, Fourteenth Report; *Reform of Judicial Administration* (Vol. I, Chapters 1-29), Ministry of Law, Government of India, New Delhi, 1958.

participants in the said convention viewed this step on the part of Government as a blatant interference with the rights, prerogatives and independence of the lawyers themselves i.e. both judges and lawyers. As such, it posed according to them, a grave threat and challenge to the whole professional collectivity and called for a united and concerted stand to meet this challenge. Hence, a convention was organized in Vigyan Bhavan, New Delhi on 11-12 August, 1973.

As already stated, the participants debated this issue not so much as an issue in itself as in relation to the politico-ideological set-up in the country as well as to the ruling government's attitude towards it and judiciary. Accordingly, we have classified the cognitions as under:

(*i*) *Cognitions about Systemic Reality*

The participants stressed again and again that India was a democracy characterized by certain fundamental rights which constituted its substantive ideological core.

> "". . .A Society which believes in certain basic rights normally turns to a democratic form of government which in itself ensures the freedom of the members of that society, and seeks to ensure this objective through the Rule of Law."

'Rule of law' in the lawyers' perception is the logical extension or rather the operational denominator of democracy, so that, to damage it, would amount to impairing the whole system. One also noticed a repeated attempt by participants to provide a *contemporary* ideological anchorage to the 'Rule of Law' and bracket it with 'socialism.'

> ". . .What is the first postulate of democracy ? Surely the postulate of Socialism. . .I am talking of socialism in a democratic manner, the first postulate of socialism is the Rule of Law."

It was then towards the realization of this basic objective of strengthening the Rule of Law in society that separation of powers between the three organs of the state, namely the Legislature, the Executive and the Judiciary was thought to be incapable.

> "...The doctrine of separation of powers has its highest validity in respect of the independence of the judiciary from the Executive and the Legislature."

Once, separation of powers was accepted as a constitutional principle and as principle of political governance, it was automatic, as the lawyers perceived, that judiciary would assume a corrective function with repect to both Executive and Legislature.

> "It is the function of judiciary to deal fairly with those who may exceed their power in appointed areas... This could no doubt be corrected by political methods, either constitutional or revolutionary. In the first case, redress is slow and no individual may get relief during his own life time or at all. The second is not an ordinary phenomenon and may well defeat its very objective. It is the judiciary alone that can correct the legislature or Executive excesses or encroachments. The Executive in any country often tends to exceed its just and legitimate limits of jurisdiction. This is not unnatural but the people who have been assured of certain freedoms have to turn to the Judiciary for the preservation of their freedoms, because in the nature of things neither agency can serve the purpose."

Judiciary's prerogative is not only to exercise 'corrective' function *vis-a-vis* the other two organs, but also to correct itself.

> "... It is the function of Judiciary to correct the excesses and irregularities not only of the Legislature and of the Executive but of the Judiciary itself as where the lower courts tend to error and even when the highest court of the land finds that the realities of the situation at a given period of time require that it should consider afresh and if need be, review its own decisions to bring its verdict in consonance with the basic rights of the people in the context of the times."

It is interesting that none of the various speakers perceived the apparent anomaly between Judiciary's capacity's to correct Executive and Legislature on the one hand, and to correct and regulate its own functioning, on the other. How would this professionally vested criticality operate so omnisciently as to perform such vastly diverse functions as criticizing or monitoring 'others' and also itself ? Or, in other words, is it not necessary to think of some independent controls and mechanisms required for ensuring intra-professional criticality ? Further, as the above quote shows, the lawyers perceived 'irregularities' as mostly associated with the functioning of the lower courts and not the higher courts, the assumption being that even though professional admonishing of the lower courts could be done by the higher courts for their irregularities, the higher courts themselves needed no such censures or correctives. We do admit that this unequal power wielded by the higher courts *vis-a-vis* the lower courts, is an automatic inescapable consequence of the hierarchy of courts as existing within the framework of law. But what is really puzzling is that this unwarranted assumption of the highest judiciary being able to set right its own house without any coercive or persuasive inputs from without, does not, in the least, sound untenable to those who are professionally so well-equipped to discern such oddities.

(*ii*) *Cognitions about the Political Power Milieu*

The supersession of the Supreme Court judges was not perceived as an isolated development. Rather, it revealed much deeper designs of the Government to concentrate more and more political power into its hands. As such it was also evidenced by a variety of related developments in society.

> "...If you look at the contemporary scene, there will not be any doubt in our minds that we are moving more and more towards the centralization of power, towards a monolithic stage, towards the concentration in government of everything that matters in the life of the citizens."

Further, even this trend towards over-centralization of political power was a derivative of a more general *systemic* shift being pioneered by the present government. The whole politico-ideological basis of our society, as the lawyers perceived, was being altered and subverted, in favour of a more totalitarian, dictatorial type of political system. This is how they perceived the doctrine of *social philosophy* of the judges as enunciated by the then law minister Kumaramangalam.

> "... The pernicious social philosophy is nothing but an attempt by the government to translate bodily into our structure this communist totalitarian philosophy of captive political thoughts, regimented thoughts, as we have them in the totalitarian countries." Or, "He (*i.e.* Kumaramangalam) was committed to making Indian Judicial system as a replica of the Soviet system of justice. . ."

In view of its above-mentioned 'power' and ideological, aspirations the government was seen as trying to ride roughshod over the autonomy of judiciary, which it regarded as the biggest custodian of democratic rights and therefore, as the sole hindrance in the achievement of government's designs. Thus, the supersession of the principle of 'seniority' in the case of Judges was not seen as a chance measure taken by the government, but

> "a pre-meditated, calculated attack on the independence of judiciary."

The lawyers saw in this a "sinister pattern" and a successive build-up towards a state of *insignificant* judiciary.

> "... Look at the speeches of certain political leaders, in Parliament and outside, during the last three or four years, and you will find a steady attempt to denigrade the judiciary and the great legal profession which are bulwarks of liberty and which they themselves appeal to and enlist in their support whenever they themselves are in trouble."

(*iii*) *Cognitions about Profession*

Part of professionals' perceptions about themselves have already been reported under the first section concerned with their cognition about ideological-political system in the country. It was reported above that lawyers viewed "separation of powers" and the "surveillance" function of judiciary over Legislature and Executive as axiomatic to the very perpetuation of democratic order in the country. It was also mentioned that the efficiency of judiciary to supervise Executive and Legislature as well as its own affairs was taken for granted by the lawyers. It was thus assumed that a judge will automatically start performing his role with the utmost efficiency once he occupied the position of a judge. He requires no training, no professional socialization preparing him in this role.

It is no wonder, therefore, that the above-mentioned assumptions of self-righteousness on the part of the members of profession should lead them to thinking that their profession is cut out to play the role of "leaders" in society.

> "... It is our duty as lawyers, as the intelligentsia of the country (and that way we are in the midst of a vastly illiterate electorate perhaps more numerous than elected representations throughout the country). It is our duty to arouse public opinion from its apathy and to fight this menace of conformity. Unless this is done, I see justice enslaved, I see the rule of law reversed, and I see the walls closing in. Soon if we do not do anything. If we do not arouse public opinion by our own initiative and our example and our exhortations, we may find ourselves in one vast ghetto of restricted joyless, and regimented lives."

It is not overnight that the profession finds itself vested with the role of a leader. Rather, it has always played its pioneering role since its inception . . . especially during the country's struggle for independence.

> ". . .Time was when lawyers were in the vanguard of our struggle for freedom."

So domineering in this sense of 'historical significance' on the part of the profession that they shift back and forth on the stream of time in weird combinations of cognitions lacking historical contextuality altogether. Note the following :

> "... If Mahatma Gandhi had been alive today, he would have perhaps revived the whole Civil Disobedience movement all over again to start a *crusade* (emphasis supplied) against which we may call (to use the title of the one-time Lord Chief Justice Lord Stewarts' book in a slightly different sense). 'This new Despotism'."

(B) Law Commission Report

Whereas the preceding account dealt with deliberations of lawyers specifically called to formalise a collective stand on a specific issue of state policy, which is perceived by profession as having important bearing on the independence of judiciary, the account under this section analyses the structure of their understanding regarding a proposed institutional innovation within the legal system *viz.* of providing legal aid to the poor and indigent clients. The material used for this analysis *i. e.* the Law Commission Report of 1958, is the most authentic and representative expression of professionals' views and opinions, both of individuals as well as of various professional bodies, on the relevance of the legal aid programme, the method and mode of its implementation, its implications for the state, society and profession etc. As already argued by us in the earlier part of our paper on the structure of professional relations, the crucial determinant of the success of legal aid programme is an appropriate orientation and preparedness on the part of lawyers. Accordingly, therefore, we shall glean specific evidence on this aspect, from the relevant sections of the said report (pp. 587-624) devoted to legal aid. We shall try to map the overall cognitive pattern of the profession regarding the programme and its relationship with the rest of society. The discussion will, therefore, be arranged under : (1) The Programme and the Socio-Constitutional Setting. (2) The Programme and the State : (3) The programme and the Profession.

(*i*) *The Programme and the Socio-Constitutional Setting*

The report sees a clear continuity between the constitutionally enshrined promise of justice and equality and proposed programme of free legal aid and recognizes that equality before law necessarily presupposes some provisions which promote the accessibility of the poor and un-privileged to the law of the state.

> "... But access to the courts is by law made dependent upon the payment of the court fees, and the assistance of the skilled lawyers is in most cases necessary for the proper presentation of a party's case in a court of law. In so far as a person is unable to obtain access to a court of law for having his wrongs redressed or for defending himself against a criminal charge, justice becomes unequal and laws which are meant for his protection have no meaning and to that extent fail in their purpose. Unless some provision is made for assisting the poor man for the payment of court-fees and other incidental costs of litigation he is denied equality in the opportunity to seek justice. The rendering of legal aid to the poor litigant is, therefore not a minor problem of procedural law but a question of a fundamental character."

In espousing the relevance of the programme for the modern Indian society, the report takes cognizance of the fact that in its germinal sense, it has always been thought to be necessary and accordingly goes over the major findings of the various committees and commissions set up from time to time to review the problem—right from Trevor Harris Committee of 1949 to the latest Bhagwati Committee. The report notes that all these bodies have consensually upheld the relevance of this programme and have suggested various ways and measures of achieving the results. The report also reviews the success made by this programme in other countries of the world, such as USA, England and Canada and thus tries to reaffirm the relationship between a democratic order and the legal aid programmes.

(ii) Programme and the State

In its entire report, the law commission looks upon the proposed programme in terms of state subsidy and support to the poor and the indigent. Accordingly, instead of clients having to pay counsels' fees, the state should come forward and pay. To buttress this opinion, numerous citations have been made from various committee reports as well as scholarly writings to this effect. Note the following from E. J. Cohn :

> "... It is part of that protection of the citizen's individuality which, in our modern conception of the relations between the citizen and the state can be claimed by those citizens who are too weak to protect themselves. Just as the modern state tries to protect the poorer classes against the common dangers of life, such as unemployment, disease, old age, social oppression etc., so it should protect them when legal difficulties arise. Indeed the case for such protection is stronger than the case for any other form of protection. The state is not responsible for the outbreak of epidemics, for old age, or economic crisis. That law again is made for the protection of all citizens poor and rich alike. It is therefore the duty of the state to make its machinery work alike for the rich and the poor."[11]

It is in the light of above assumption, that explanations for the failure of the legal aid programme so far in the country in general and several states in particular, are sought in the inadequate budgetary allocations made for the purpose. The line of argument is thus quite simple : more money made available by the state for paying counsels' fees, greater would be the success of the programme.

(iii) Programme and the Profession

It is ironic that despite a forceful recognition of the inevitability of the programme for the maintenance of democratic

11. *Ibid.* p. 594. Quoted from E.J. Cohn, "Legal Aid for the Poor", *Law Quarterly Review*, Vol. LIX, pp. 250-56.

order, the Commission recommends no *specific* and *concrete* guidelines whereby the lawyers themselves may be persuaded to render free legal aid to the poor. No norms are proposed whose compliance on the part of the members should be declared obligatory by the professional bodies and brought to bear on the day-to-day functioning of the programme. In this, the right of the lawyer to charge fee from a client (and for that matter from any client—even a poor and indigent one !) is asserted.

> "A lawyer is in the same position as a qualified doctor or engineer permitted to practise his profession. If members of these latter professions or other professions may not be compelled to do professional work without payment for poor persons, there appears to be no reason why a discriminatory compulsion of any kind should be imposed on the legal profession."[12]

Further :

> "An argument which is freely used to justify the putting of the responsibility on the legal profession of rendering this service to the community gratuitously is that the legal profession having been granted important privilege in regard to the administration of the law, it is its obligation to look after the needy litigant, without charging fees. The very basis of this argument appears to us to be unsound. The profession of the law like any other profession can be adopted and practised by persons who have obtained the necessary qualification and license permitting its practice. It would thus appear to be no different from any other profession and it would be incorrect to assume that the profession has been granted any privileges in regard to the administration of law."[13]

Thus, instead of formalizing the criteria by which the professionals could assist in the programme, or instead of stressing the

12. *Op. cit.*, p. 595.
13. *Ibid.*, p. 595.

need on the part of the professional bodies to lay down certain norms for guiding the behaviour of the lawyers, the principle of "voluntarism" is invoked again and again, leaving it virtually to the whim of the individual lawyer whether to assist in the programme or not.

> "Legal assistance to the poor litigant may be rendered effectively by a member of the legal profession voluntarily undertaking such work."[14]

However, there is no dearth of exhortations, platitudes and unbounded optimism that the professionals in India, in true deference to the *grand tradition* which they possess, should assist in the implementation of the programme. Even though the report under mention is replete with such observations, the following illustration should suffice as a representative piece :

> ". . . Lawyers in India would not be worthy of the great traditions of the profession if they failed to render this *social service* (emphasis supplied) which can be so usefully and appropriately rendered by them."[15]

But despite its refusal to impose any 'coercive' or 'persuasive' controls on the professionals to make the programme a success, the Commission does not want lawyers to be left out of the programme. In other words, 'offers' are made of some useful organizational, administrative help which the lawyers can easily lend to the programme on account of their *technical expertise and knowledge.*

> ". . . The training and equipment of the lawyer, his close association with the machinery for administration of justice and his knowledge of its procedures tend to make him the fittest instrument for administering a scheme of legal aid."[16]

14. *Ibid.*, p. 595.
15. *Ibid.*, p. 597.
16. *Op. cit.*

This may be seen more as a clever device by the profession for retaining control over the administration of the scheme, ensuring maximum pay-off for its own members, rather than any genuine offer for the welfare of the poor and indigent.

IV. CONCLUSIONS : POVERTY, PROFESSIONAL DECEPTION AND SOCIAL CHANGE

(a)

As stated in the beginning of this chapter, it is possible to whittle down the rigours of poverty and social inequality for the affected people, by promoting their existential efficiency through various institutional improvisations. One such improvisation is to provide free legal aid to the poor, which in operational terms boils down to providing them with the facility of free legal representation in a court of law. It is quite apparent that in case this help reaches the needy people in a genuine measure, the poor would have lost one crippling disadvantage they face *vis-a-vis* the rich in our society which is marked by sharply stratified life opportunities. To that extent, therefore, we would have taken a giant stride towards egalitarianism—through the successful implementation of legal aid programme.

We also noted above that despite all the optimism that goes with the programme of free legal aid, the crucial link in this whole process of social causation is the legal professional or the lawyer who must play a very crucial and determining part in implementing the programme 'genuinely'. In other words, it is only through a clear and strong pro-poor orientation of the lawyer that the programme can become a success. This, we noted was so because of the comprehensive dependence of clients on their counsels in all aspects of litigation—a fact which the counsels are so used to exploiting for their pecuniary benefits. Further, we had also surmised, that this asymmetry or inequality of relationship between the lawyer and his client automatically imposes certain limitations on the effectivity of the legal aid plan. As a result, the professional has to be genuinely compelled from within by some internalized professional ethos, norms or values, to render legal help to the poor clients.

The two sets of empirical evidence in the preceding part of the paper were intended to identify the said *potential* in the lawyers' cognitive structures *i.e.* the way they relate themselves to some emergent issues and problems entailing new demands on their professional role performance and also to the overall socio-political framework and reality.

The evidence examined brings out in bold relief complete lack of self criticality on the part of professionals both when they express themselves individually and severally as well as when they do so in the midst of a professional collectivity. The situation remains the same also when they take cognizance of a governmental measure having direct or indirect bearing on their profession, its autonomy etc., and also when they formalize their collective response to a newly proposed plan tending to change or broaden the ambit of their professional role performance.

First and the foremost feature of their cognitive structure as emerging from the above case-studies is that the lawyers perceive themselves as central to the existing socio-political reality, the entire scheme of things in society. As judiciary they are the watch-dogs of constitutional proprieties, whether these concern the functioning of Legislature, Executive or the Judiciary itself. Not only that, they also perceive themselves as having rendered a crucial role in the making of the contemporary Indian history. Further, it is not only with regard to the constitution or to the present and past of the Indian society that lawyers perceive themselves as having played important role, but they also visualize themselves as having been cast to lead the illiterate millions to their progress. This is so because, being the 'intelligentsia' they are their undisputed leaders.

Secondly, they perceive an attitude of strong hostility on the part of government towards them. In fact, this cognition flows from the earlier one in that, sensing that legal professionals are the main obstacle between their monoply over political power and the people, the government is sparing no opportunity of weakening and humiliating judiciary. The judiciary on granted assumption that the state will provide for the counsels' fees and also in view of the well known paucity of business available to the lawyers, especially those with little experience and practice to their credit, seems to advance the cause of the not-too happily placed lawyers. Indirectly, therefore, the net result of these suggestions, if accepted, would be to romote the employment—potential of the "needy" and briefless lawyers. What else it is then a trade unionist trickstery?

(b)

The analysis so far reveals that the professional cognitions lack self-criticality or reflexivity about the conditions of their practice and recognition of any serious responsibility for rendering professional assistance to the poor—a responsibility which really falls within their own professional domain. When such a state of professional cognitions is supplemented by inequitous professional relations, in which lawyers exercise immense power over their clients through mystique of their technical expertise, then any hope of a *genuine* professional assistance reaching the poor and the indigent is killed in its very offing. Unless, therefore, a professional's personality is prepared differently through a much more self-critical socialization and a consequent assimilation of a *radical ethos*, professional assistance would exist more in claim than in reality. And, the required thrust for such a fundamental transformation in professional perceptions and cognitions can possibly come only from professional bodies which should promote appropriate attitudes and values among their constituent members for the promotion of free professional assistance. That, this is not a mere platitude but a realistic possibility is easily proved if one goes over the recent history of legal aid movement in America and Britain where various bar organisations have played a highly significant role in developing radically different role-orientations among the lawyers.[17]

But, given the genre of legal professional that we have at present in the country—whether in practice as lawyer or sitting

17. *Op. cit.*

on the bench, it would be foolhardy to expect that they could be genuinely involved in the alleviation of poverty. Ideally, of course, it should be left to the lawyers themselves to devise ways and means whereby the poor and indigent can be brought at par with the rich through professional support and assistance. But the guild-minded, self-righteous and exploitative professional that emerges from the preceding analysis, should be singularly unfit to conceive of any legal aid plan and to execute it upto any semblance of effectivity. The propensity to exploit that is rooted in the very structure of professional relations, gets all the more whetted by the keenly competitive conditions of practice. As a result, any 'manifest' attempt on the part of profession to look 'concerned' about poor clients is far from genuine and is meant only as a public posture—*i.e.* to prevent it from appearing unconcerned with some important public issue. On the other hand, the profession finds itself in the crucible of history where its task is to stay the hands of the government which is concentrating increasingly more powers into its own hands and thus taking society towards Soviet-type totalitarianism.

Thirdly, the profession reacts with furious intensity to any suggestions for curbing its independence, whether concerning its own internal functioning or concerning its interaction with the outside world. That is why, the appointment of the Judiciary is resented even though government itself is the appointing authority under the law. Also, any suggestion for formalizing a programme whereby lawyers could be persuaded to render free legal aid is rejected by them.

Whereas it is possible to understand why the members of a profession refuse to be contained in their professional autonomy, one is at pains to understand why the professional collectivity lacks the urge to spell out some norms for the guidance of their constituent members in the legal aid programme. In fact, the members of a profession enjoy autonomy *vis-a-vis* the rest of society only because they are able to evolve their own norms to which they adhere in their day-to-day professional conduct and practice. But, as against this, the professionals under examination here, while rejecting the imposition of any outside norms and criteria such as the requirement of a certain *social philosophy* in the appointment of Supreme Court Judges, also reject that the professional bodies themselves evolve formal norms for orienting their members to promote the legal aid programme.

So intense is their desire to keep away from any, 'impecunious' commitment to the poor clients that through a forceful argument the *profession* is sought to be equated with an ordinary *economic enterprise* where 'profit' and 'payoff' is natural and inescapable : This brings out clearly, a pure and simple, trade-unionist mentality of professional leaders who try to achieve the maximum benefits for their constituents at the minimum cost.

This impression is buttressed all the more by some more evidence. Firstly, the responsibility for running and financing the legal aid plan is put exclusively on the shoulders of the state despite a clear recognition of its incapacity to bear this burden. Secondly, even though backing out of any financial commitments by way of providing free assistance to the poor clients, they still consider it necessary—because of their technical expertise, that they are coopted into the administration of the plan. The suggestion, in fact, means nothing else than that lawyers be allowed to *control* and *steer* this programme, securing whatever benefits possible to their own profession. As our anaysis abundantly shows, one does not need to fall back upon any indirect proof or use *inferential* logic to perceive the mythical or deceptive character of their 'concerns' and claims. The entire structure of their cognitions which is nothing but negativistic and evasive, speaks volumes for this inference.

(c)

What happens if the programme of legal aid is still pursued despite the fact that profession undergoes no radicalization of its ethos and passes no new sensitivities to its members ? It is easy to see that the resulting consequence will not only be the subversion of programme and the attendant aggrandizement of the profession at a huge social and financial cost, but also the reification of professional mystique—to which only the clients are susceptible hitherto, into an enduring structure of popular *deception*. In other words, a false sense of hope would now come to descend upon the wider society—inclusive of those who *legislate, plan* and *execute* on behalf of the people. As professional improprieties, on the part of the lawyers continue to flourish, we can expect endless permutations of *spurious* rather than *genuine* services from them, of needless multiplication of litigation engaged in by the people. This myth is likely to be perpetuated all the more, simply because it is the profession itself which is going to adjudge the efficiency of service rendered to a poor client. Ivan Illich is right in pointing out that professions exercise an unlimited degree of control over human life through their very power to structure human needs and then to structure their fulfilment.[18] The need to litigate for the sake of one's right is now sought to be fulfilled within the legal aid programme which is proposed, designed and directed by those who constitute the powerful *interest group* within the legal system.[19] The outcome is thus likely to be anything but the welfare of the poor and indigent !

The obvious question is why and how this autonomy to structure the legal aid programme has worked positively in certain cases—for example, in American and British society. The answer is simple : The profession in both these countries—as a composite of lawyers and Judiciary, has worked much more self-consciously and critically in evolving various norms and criteria and then prevailed upon their constituents to follow them in practice. It is the first lesson in sociological thinking that norms are a collective product and also that, in order to cause social change, new inner compulsions in the form of new norms have to be generated among the individuals by the respective collectivities controlling their behaviour.[20] In the case of lawyers, such collectivities are professional bodies which are 'expected' to play a

18. Ivan Illich, *et. al* (eds.) *The Disabling Professions*, Middlesex, Penguine, 1977.

19. A similar argument is employed in author's earlier paper.

20. Emile Durkheim, *Professional Ethics and Civic Morals*, New York, Free Press of Glencoe, 1958.

permanent role in the socialization and recruitment of lawyers into the professional behaviour. Only if and when this happens, profession would play a positive role in the alleviation of poverty and trigger the process of genuine social change.

CHAPTER FOUR

SOCIAL NETWORKS, PROFESSIONAL CHOICE AND SOCIAL CHANGE : A PERSPECTIVE ON DISTRICT COURT LAWYERS

I. INTRODUCTION : THE STUDY, METHODOLOGY ETC.

THE PRESENT CHAPTER is based upon my doctoral work; "Lawyers at a District Court : A Study in the Sociology of Legal Profession", which in a modified manner has already been published.[1] In addition, it substantially draws upon the data on the 'patterns of professional choice-making, which did not form part of either the doctoral work or the book mentioned above—even though these were also collected as a part of the same investigations. The core-argument which is sought to be built up here on the strength of the data is that social networks of the lawyers practising at the district court in question; viz., Gobindgarh, make a comprehensive contribution towards professional practice inclusive of the process of professional choice-making, recruitment, professional mobility or career-making. This, as we have tried to argue in this chapter underscores some of the basic incongruities between the conceptual construct of professions on the one hand and the social reality in which the profession of our study is anchored, on the other. A basic rationale is thus available for re-thinking or a re-conceptualization of professions as a category of analysis. In addition, as we have tried to show, this also highlights the inappropriateness of the legal profession to play any meaningful role in facilitating the process of social change in the Indian Society.

1. J.S. Gandhi, *Lawyers and Touts : A Study in the Sociology of Legal Profession*, Hindustan Publishing Corporation, New Delhi, 1982.

The field-work for this study was carried out in a district court of Punjab and spread between 1973-76. A variety of respondents were interviewed, which included lawyers, their clerks (called *munshis*), clients, a variety of court employees and para-employees such as stamp-vendors, petition-writers, typists etc., and also touts i.e. those mercenary suppliers of legal business who mediate between the lawyers and their clients. Our main instrument of inquiry was *unstructured interview*, combined with on-the-spot observations of various respondents in their mutual interaction. In addition, several group-interviews were also carried out as well as several sessions of lawyers' group-gossip observed and analysed to identify the dynamics of their professional functioning. Some of the court records—especially those relating to the nature and number of cases decided as well as relating to courts' evolution over the last eighty years or so were also read through.

In the account which follows, we shall first provide a theoretical backdrop to the specific issue of our study and explore the relevance of social network connections in the pursuit of professional practice within the framework of theory of professions. In other words, how far the reality of professions as available to us from our impirical observations fits into the conceptual construct of professions. Subsequently, we shall also explore the potentials of the profession of our study to play any meaningful role in the process of social change.

II. THEORETICAL BACKDROP

The evolution of professions in every society has been necessarily accompanied by the process of secularisation, which in the context of European societies has meant the progressive liberation of professions from Church and its control. That is to say, professions achieved a progressive autonomy vis-a-vis the Church which earlier was the source-spring of personnel required for these professions. This process is particularly relevant with regard to the profession of Law and Medicine. The integral expertise required of a member of ministry was at one time inclusive of the expertise to diagnose and treat the physical ailments as well as the proficiency to know, interpret and apply state law to a variety of discrete situations. In the said process of secularisation which continued over the years, one can see anticipations of *professional autonomy* which later came to be accepted as the corner-stone of professional practice.

However, in the subsequent evolution of professions—notably the Law and Medicine, secularization also came to denote a de-linking between religious belongingness on the one hand and the right to join and pursue a certain profession, on the other. In its place was now required a specific professional expertise and competence. One comes across this trend of progressive secularisation even in the evolution of Indian legal profession.[2]

It needs to be particularly emphasized that *modern* legal profession did not arise in India in response to certain indigenous conditions and circumstances. Instead, it was implanted here by the British only as a logical consequence of the extension and establishment of the British rule.

Further, at the time of the transference to India, legal profession had already undergone a substantial refinement in terms of *secularisation, professional autonomy* and *role specificity* in the land of its origin i.e. the British society, so much so that it nearly approximated the theoretical construct of professions we recognize it today.

But, despite the above-mentioned historical distinctiveness of legal profession in India, it did undergo secularization associated with it in the west. In other words, the right to qualify for and practise law was thrown open, only progressively, to people from all religions and castes. Further, as it has been in the case of

2. "Even though the Bengal Regulation VII of 1793 and its subsequent extension to other states, which regulated the appointment of *vakils* or native pleaders in the court of civil judicature, had an extraordinary provision whereby only Muslims and Hindus could be enrolled as pleaders. The situation continued till 1806 when the Punjab Chief Courts Act waived any such discrimination between various communities. Under this Act, any person duly authorised by the Secretary of State for India in Council to appear, could plead or act on his behalf (Quoted from the original act in : Report of the All India Bar Committee, Indian Government, Ministry of Law, New Delhi," : cited in J.S. Gandhi, *Ibid.*, 31).

legal professions in the west, legal education in India too; has undergone a corresponding secularisation, which means that, as the profession evolved, religious texts ceased to supply the substantive core of professional education. Instead, an independent body of knowledge constitutive of contemporary state law, came to be accepted as the basis of professional training and education. The brief discussion in the proceeding section leads us to a clear inference that *secularism* has been inseparably associated with the growth of *professionalism* both in India and in the West.

In the contemporary sociological theory, one comes across a related expression. i.e. *Universalism*, to refer to one of the three fundamental attributes of modern professions—the other two being *specificity* and *rationality*.[3] The argument is that professions being a characteristic product of the modern societies partake of their fundamental characteristics, which are universalism, specificity and rationality. It would indeed be a rewarding exercise to examine the extent of fit or incongruence between the above elucidations of professional attributes and the empirical reality of professional practice as brought out in over study. For the present paper, we have undertaken this exercise—but only with regard to one of its three attributes i.e. *universalism*. But, before we proceed further, let us note what *universalism* specifically denotes within the context of modern profession. One of the pioneers of this concept —Talcott Parsons avers :

> It is one of the most striking features of our occupational system that status in it is to a high degree independent of status in kinship groups, the neighbourhood and the like, in short from what are sometimes called primary group relationships. It may be suggested that one of the main reasons for this lies in the dominant importance of universalistic criteria in the judgement of achievement in the occupational field.[4]

It may be seen here that the connotation of universalism extends beyond secularization so as to imply absence or complete lack of

3. Talcott Parsons, The Professions and Social Structure in his *Essays in Sociological Theory* (rev. edn.) Glancoe, Ill; The Free Press, 1954, pp. 34-49.
4. *Ibid.*

primary ties and relationships in the professional role-discharge and professional career-making, which is to say that a professional's status should not be contingent upon his ties in his primary milieux. Rather, it would follow from the skill and merit of his professional performance. As against all such 'theoretic' stipulations, the data we have here goes convincingly to show that professional's *intimate network-resources* play a crucial role in all sectors of professional functioning. As a result, it virtually becomes inescapable to identify the profession in terms of various primary ties and network-connections. As a result we, have a *profession* which is a *non-profession* in its functional sense if we regard *universalism* as one of its core-characteristics. In the succeeding section of this chapter, we shall discuss the nature of this evidence and draw its implications for the ideal-typical theoretical construct of professions. We shall also consider the relevance of these implications for the legal professsion's ability to plan an effective role in the process of social change—especially in the context of Third World countries.

III. PROFESSIONAL CHOICE-MAKING

Operationally, the term "professional, choice-making" in our study has been used to refer to the process of joining graduation-course in law, even though all those who join the course and complete it may not end up in legal practice. Instead, many of them may find their way into some administrative and technical careers either in private or public establishments. For example, nearly all the young lawyers below the age of 25, were candidates either for the Indian Administrative Services Examination or for the State Judicial Service. All this can be appreciated in the light of very difficult circumstances that a practitioner has to go through in the initial phase of his career when he has very little or no business to support himself. Yet, our decision to operationally restrict the term *professional choice* to one's *entry into professional education*, can be defended on the ground that on the completion of law-graduation, Lawyer's career is the most apparent opening that one has before oneself.

'How did you decide to join graduation course in law,' was the approximate formulation of the question put to the legal practitioners in the course of un-structured yet focussed interviews. In reply, they were persuaded to identify the most important influence or influences that had been operative towards this choice. Even though, the question was focussed at all the 154 practitioners at Gobindgarh Courts (fictitious name), only in 125 cases could we obtain the desired information. Following table reports the results.

The succeeding table analyses and classified practitioners' perception of such significant factors or influences as were responsible for their going into professional education. As is obvious, of the total 125 cases, the respondents were themselves responsible for the professional choice only in 14 per cent cases. Further, the largest

TABLE : *Showing "Most Important Influence" that operated upon professional choice-making.*

Category of influence	*Frequency*	*Percentage*
1. Self-directed choices	18	14
2. Father-directed choices	52	42
3. 'Other' directed choices	25	20
4. Career-guided choices	30	24
	125	100

single category i.e. 42 per cent belonged to those who were goaded into law by their fathers. If we break up the third category of *'other'—directed choices* into further sub-classifications, we get the following picture :

Choices mediated through Ego :	20	15%
Choices mediated through Ego's father :	5	5%
	25	

That is to say, twenty out of twenty five practitioners as listed in the above table under category 3, were themselves influenced by persons other than their own fathers which included— in order of importance, ego's own brothers, his mother's brother, his father's brother, his father-in-law or the latter's brother. In other words, another twenty or 8 per cent of the total career choices were also influenced by ego's close network-kinship or affinal. Finally, therefore, we may say that at least in half of the total cases, the decision to go into professional career was not that of the practitioner himself but of those persons located in his close and intimate social network. Thus, career-choice making here should mean a substantially different entity from what it means in most of the western literature on occupational choice, since in the latter, it mostly implies *choice exerted by the incumbant himself* and not by his father, family or social network.[5]

This characteristic feature of professional choice-making we think, would be applicable to the choice of occupation or career anywhere in the Indian society because of the simple reason that family, parents and kins continue to matter importantly in a variety of decisions in the individual's life-especially till the time that he is not economically self-reliant. Father dominates not only the occupational decision-making in the life of an Indian youth, but also provides him full maintenance till such time that he starts earning his own livelihood. All this needs to be appreciated also in the overall context of yet resilient joint family system in India, which survives in the midst of several "hostile" forces such as progressive industrialization and urbanization of society.

The evidence on the role of intimate social networks in the structure and functioning of legal profession as supplied above gets corroborated if we consider the social background of the practitioners under study. The operational denominator here for the social background is the occupational background of the lawyers' fathers.

---

5. On this point, the following illustrations would suffice, in view of the very few empirical studies available in this area of occupational choice :
   (i) Eli Ginzberg *et al.*, *Occupational Choice : An Approach to a General Theory*, New York, Columbia University Press, 1951.
   (ii) Robert K. Merton *et al.*, *The Student Physician*, Cambridge : Massachusetts, Harvard University Press, 1969.

TABLE : *Occupational Background of Gobindgarh Lawyers' Fathers*

Occupational background	*Frequency*	*Percentage*
1. Business	39	25.3
2. Law and law-related	39	25.3
3. Farming	31	20.1
4. White-collar occupations	22	14.2
5. Teaching	15	9.7
6. Not available	5	3.2
7. Ritualistic (priestly etc.)	5	1.9
	154	99.7

The above table reveals that a substantial number of practitioners i.e. 49.2 per cent (collapsing categories 1, 4, 5) were drawn from either professions—i.e. law or teaching, or from white-collar occupations—whether in public or private establishments. Another major category is 'business' which supplies another one-fourth (25.3 per cent) of the total bar. This goes in correspondence with the fact that civil practice has the highest concentration of practitioners at Gobindgarh district courts. The upshot of all this information is that most of the professional recruitment takes place from professionals themselves, or from the middle or upper middle class background—which in a net sense amounts to the negation of *universalism*—the ideal-typical characteristic of professionalism.

IV. PROFESSIONAL MOBILITY

The predominance of particularistic ties and connections in the legal profession is evidenced not only in professional choice-making and in the social bases of professional recruitment, but also in the process of career-mobility. We discovered that, other things being equal, lawyers with intimate network resources advanced farther and quicker in their professional career than those who were without them. But, before we furnish data to support this contention, we must report some relevant facts on the phenomenon of professional hierarchy as it obtained at Gobindgarh courts during our period of study.

In all, we identified three areas of practice : Civil, Criminal and Revenue at Gobindgarh courts. This classification is at once exhaustive in the empirical sense as well as subjectively relevant in that it corresponds to the way practitioners themselves, define and perceive the whole range of practice at the district courts as constitutive of those three divisions. Using 'exclusiveness' of practice in any one of the areas to the exclusion of the other areas on the part of lawyers, we identified the following three categories of practitioners in the district court under study.

1. Exclusive Lawyers
2. Semi-Exclusive Lawyers.
3. Non-Exclusive Lawyers.

Accordingly, Exclusive lawyers were those who did not accept a 'brief' from outside their own area of specialization—whether civil, criminal or revenue. They had at least three decades of professional experience to their credit or even more.

Semi-Exclusive lawyers were those who practised in two of the three practice-areas. Even so, one of these two could be identified as their *predominant* or *primary* area which was responsible for anywhere between sixty to eighty percent of their total business, whereas the other could be regarded as *secondary* or *subsidiary*. The largest number of Semi-Exclusive lawyers i.e. 65 per cent had a regular stay in the profession for a period ranging between 11 and 25 years.

As for the Non-Exclusive lawyers, they drew from all the practice-areas indiscriminately with a view to get adequate business to live by. It is important to note that both in terms of intra-professional estimations, as well as in terms of earnings, Exclusive lawyers could be ranked at the top and the Non-Exclusives at the bottom with the semi-exclusives in between. The largest proportion among Non-exclusives, 74 per cent had professional experience ranging from a few months to 9-10 years.

An important theoretical implication of the above categorization is that specialization in a certain area of practice to the progressive exclusion of other areas is an important attribute of upward career-mobility. In other words, through a prolonged stay in profession, a lawyer tends to develop increasingly specialized practice and through charging a relatively higher fee per case, achieve upward career-mobility in the professional hierarchy. It is important to note that this formulation goes against a predominant view which regards practice at a district court as essentially indiscriminate and un-differentiated.[6]

Even though, the preceding sections of the chapter independently establish the importance of network connections in legal profession, their crucial test would be in whether or not they have any bearing on the structure and process of professional hierarchy as identified by us above. In other words, the crucial question worth pursuing should be whether or not a professional achieves 'exclusive' category relatively quicker through the benefit of network connections. For this, we started by identifying the time-span of practice in the case of twelve lawyers who figured in the Exclusive category. This worked out to 29-45 years. We now controlled for this time-span and identified a total of 33 lawyers in the district courts which also included the twelve lawyers already figuring in the Exclusive category. So the question which automatically arises is what happened to the remaining 21 lawyers ? Why did they not find their place among the Exclusives ?

First of all, as many as 17 among these had migrated from Pakistan into Gobindgarh after the partition of 1947. As such they had no local connections to supply them business and help them

6. This inference from our study regarding the specialization in practice as *germane* to the nature and character of legal profession at a district court, goes counter to an uncritical acceptance of *non-specialization* in practice as the hallmark of district court practice in some scholarly circles. (e.g. Charles Morrison, "Social Organization at the District Courts : Colleague Relationships among Indian Lawyers", *Law and Society Review*, Vol. 3, Nos. 2-3, November 1968-February 1969, p. 261.) This view is not only fallacious but also static since it refuses to take into view one of the significant processes of career-making in the legal profession.

build up their career. In other words, they had no advantage of intimate network resources which could have provided a suitable fillip to their careers in the initial as well as subsequent stages of growth. The remaining four lawyers, even though based in the district in terms of their social background, had no kins or affines, to help them with business.

The following information about the network-connections of Exclusive lawyers makes our argument all the more strong and categorical.

TABLE : *Nature of Contacts available to the Exclusive lawyers from the start of their professional career*

Caste Identification	*Length of continuous practice*	*Practice area*	*Types of connections available since the beginning of the career*			
			Kindred	*Affinal*	*Native*	*Career based*
Khatri	42	Criminal	/	X	X	/
Khatri	37	Criminal	/	X	X	X
Brahmin	30	Criminal	/	X	X	X
Jatsikh	29	Criminal	X	X	/	/
Arora	30	Criminal	/	X	/	X
Arora	36	Criminal	/	/	X	X
Khatri	35	Revenue	X	X	X	X
Khatri	45	Revenue	X	/	X	X
Bania	45	Revenue	/	X	X	X
Arora	36	Civil	/	X	X	X
Bania	35	Civil	/	X	X	X
Arora	33	Civil	/	X	X	X

Available : /
Not Available : X

The above table speaks for itself. "Kindreds" constitute the single most important factor associated with the elites of the professional hierarchy in 10 out 12 cases. This was supplemented only marginally by a thin sprinkle of other contacts such as affinal ties, native-connections and career-based connections. Further, in 7 out of 12 cases kindreds were solely and exclusively responsible for maintaining a regular supply of business to the Exclusives.

Of the four non-migrant 'senior' lawyers identified above i.e. those who had a total of three to four decades of stay in the profession, but had yet failed to make the grade for the Exclusive category, only one had been supplied business through his "kindred" contacts, the remaining three having been serviced through all varieties of non-kindred contacts ranging from affinal and peer-group contacts to those that the lawyers had cultivated contextually i.e. located within the court itself among minor court-officials or other instrumental functionaries such as typists, deed-writers etc. The one with kindred contacts has had a chequered career, falling in and out of profession every few years. As a result, he could not sustain, or further expand, the volume of business accretions from these contacts.

One obvious conclusion of discussion under the section is that, in the promotion of professional career, kindred-contacts play an invaluable role and also that these contacts need to be sustained and cultivated through an un-interrupted practices at the same milieu i.e. at the same courts. The latter proposition is validated by the 13 migrant lawyers who despite their saniority in experience did not figure in the Exclusive category.

V. LAWYERS' MUNSHIS

Another very significant finding of our study has been that the lawyers practising at the district court level, are assisted in the discharge of their role by their assistants called *munshis*, in the local parlance. So significant and comprehensive is the range of services rendered by them that it virtually becomes impossible to speak of a lawyer's practice or his professional career without taking stock of his *munshi's* contribution. It is because of this reason that we have chosen to designate munshis as lawyers' ***role-subordinates*** instead of calling them merely as assistants. We have identified three main functions rendered by them : Routine Maintenance, Strategy Making and Business Promotion. All these functions are very integral and vital to the practice of a lawyer and their importance increases as a lawyer climbs higher and higher in his professional ladder. For example, it would be absolutely unrealistic to maintain that a lawyer can look after his day-to-day business routines such as keeping track of his court-calender, keeping papers for various briefs in a state of readiness and also prepare his arguments for the defence and protection of his clients. All the more ridiculous would it be to imagine that he can engage himself in a variety of professional improvisations such as trying to know or anticipate strategy of his adversary-lawyer or tutoring his witnesses before their appearance in the court. A patent line of argument on the munshi's role has so far been that it is nothing but instrumental and can be entrusted to anybody for money. But, looking to the fact that the destiny of a case in a court of law hinges precariously on the strategy involved in its preparation, the spade-work and background-work that precedes it, we can hardly dismiss munshi's role as unimportant, instrumental or dispensable.[7]

The last of the above-stated three functions i.e. business promotion, is most important of all and concerns the very survival of lawyer as a professional. This is so because a munshi acts as an important source of business-supply to his lawyer. This he achieves by garnering and exploiting his own social network—both intimate i.e. kinship-based and affinal, as well as one that is relatively distantiated such as based in co-territoriality with the clients. As an operational strategy, he vouches for the professional expertise of a certain lawyer to a prospective client and persuades him to engage his lawyer for defending his interests in a court of law. We identified in our study, an almost unvarying relationship between the contact-worthiness of a munshi and the professional status of his lawyer-employer. As a result, there comes about

7. Gandhi, *op. cit.*

a synchronic summation of the social contact-resources of a munshi and his lawyer-employer. In other words, a munshi who could draw relatively larger business from his contacts chose to work with a lawyer who—as compared to some of his other colleagues, had a larger fund of contact-resources.[8] Following response from an Exclusive lawyer sums up this situation in a characteristic manner :

> "I make no secret of the fact that I have rarely employed a munshi without considering his utility in bringing business... All of them have mattered so much for my success. At the same time, they have always had their due from me. 'H' has been very useful to me as a munshi. He has been with me for the last eighteen years. He is an important man in and around his native village and has brought me scores of cases from his friends and acquaintances...they all trust him..."

It is vivid from the discussion under this section that a variety of *particularistic* ties drawn from lawyer's own and his assistants' network are instrumental in building up his practice and in promoting his career. In other words, the level of professional achievement is in direct proportion to the volume of network-resources available to the lawyers. All this contravenes the theoretically stipulated constituent of *universalism*, according to which,

> "...status in it (i.e. profession) is to a high degree independent of status in the kinship groups, the neighbourhood and the like, in short what are sometimes called primary group relationships..."[9]

VI. CONCLUSIONS : SOCIAL NETWORKS AND SOCIAL CHANGE

We shall divide considerations under this section in two areas : Firstly, we shall try to identify some of the salient attributes of the

8. *Ibid.*
9. Talcott Parsons, *op. cit.*

lawyers i.e. their professional personality from the data supplied in the preceding. Secondly, we shall consider their suitability to play any meaningful role in the process of social change, as sought to be promoted through national planning in the country. It is implied, however, that the goals set out for social change, to bring about an egalitarian—equalitarian society, are 'proper' or 'legitimate' and 'ought to be facilitated', so that, to the extent, the lawyers in question facilitate their achievement, their contribution can be regarded as positive.

(i)

Let us first consider the general characteristics of the lawyers' professional personality as emerging from our previous account. The most obvious feature of these district court lawyers is that they are comprehensively anchored in their particularistic nexus. The process of professional entry on the part of a lawyer is spurred by his particularistic network with the anticipation that all this can be tapped latter for building up his business-base. In other words, there is a clear and obvious awareness of the crucial value of contacts, network etc., which can motivate a perspective client to engage a certain lawyer. The conclusion, therefore, is obvious that, if the said network-contacts were not there, the individual would not have been emboldened to venture into legal profession. This looks plausible in view of 'high' cost of professional education and also that the professional education is supported by the parents or family of the incumbent, so that the latter will carefully, weigh the cost of professional education vis-a-vis the perceived potentiality of social contacts to fetch business. This argument is strengthened all the more once we realize that in majority of cases, the first beneficiary of the new entrant's professional income for a few years of his professional career (at least till the time he gets married), happens to be his family. There is thus, all the more a reason for the latter to be guided by the availability of certain business-worthy contacts in the professional choices of their younger members.

It also comes out from the preceding account that the nucleus of network-contacts continues to wield a preponderant influence all along the professional career. As a result, more *intimate* is the nature of these contacts, quicker is the career-mobility of a particular lawyer. So much so, that the lawyers who are supplied contacts by their kindreds are sure to climb upto the crest of the professional hierarchy i.e. the Exclusive category in due course.

The all-pervading influences of the network resources is buttressed all the more by the summation of professional's own contacts with those of his assistant (munshi). The rationale of engaging one munshi as against another, on the part of a lawyer, is guided exclusively by the munshi's capability of ploughing his own social network resources into his lawyer's practice.

It is, therefore, obvious that the legal practice as identified by us at the district court level is built up crucially *around* and *through* network-resources, without which the substantive core of professional role performance would remain un-explained. To the extent, this picture extends to a large number of lawyers practising at other district courts in the country, professional practice can be seen to be heavily anchored in particularistic milieux. All this places the *profession* in a situation of self-contradiction, because ideal-typically, it is supposed to be independent of all varieties of primary, particularistic ties (Parsons; *Ibid.*). This inconsistency is not merely of theoretical relevance, viz. that between a conceptual construct and empirical reality. Rather, this can be seen to be damaging for the lawyers' relations vis-a-vis their clients which now, no longer remain direct and personal, but are rather mediated by all varieties of social network ties. This cuts at the very root of professional role-commitment whereunder transactions between a client and lawyer are expected to be direct, personal and independent of any persuasions or solicitings.

(ii)

In view of the above inferences, it is relevant to consider, to what extent, the professional personality of an average district court lawyer as a composite of particularistic ties and orientations, is suitable for any meaningful participation in the process of social change. But, before we do that, let us consider some of the crucial denominators of the said social change planning in the country.

The twin-emphasis on the redressal and removal of poverty and inequality is implicit in all documents of the Indian planning. Thus, all the goals and objectives as defined under various plans, have the putative consequence of alleviating poverty as well as removing the existing socio-economic polarities and inequalities. This is also clear from the fact that the sole criterion adopted for evaluating the performance of these plans is invariably in terms of economic betterment and equitable distribution of existing resources.

Under the circumstances, a lawyer can play appropriate role only if he chooses to use his professional expertise for the promotion and furtherance of the interests of under-privileged and the underdogs. This implies side-stepping market rationality of *demand and supply* and sometimes even incuring a deliberate economic disadvantage for a cause one holds professionally dear. But before one can expect such a "revolutionary" behaviour from a lawyer it is important to spell out the necessary transformation which his professional outlook must undergo before the said professional excellence can be achieved.

It may be pointed out at the very outset that "poverty" "inequity" and "deprivation"—the hallmarks of a Third World country are objective constructs and can be assimilated with a relative ease by one who is nurtured on *universalistic* ethos. A professional whose very perception of professional choice, professional practice and professional career-mobility are structured and bounded in terms of social-network resources would find it hard—if not, impossible, to extend his professional role commitment to such objective categories of clients as *indigent*, *deprived* or those suffering from socio-cultural inequities. Granting the validity of the general sociological theorem that there always is a certain inherent continuity between the social conditions and characteristics of a work milieu, and the type of cognition it generates, one may have to bemoan the basic indequacy of professional (legal) personality understudy to play any meaningful role in the midst of such imponderables as poverty, inequity, injustice etc.

Any programme, therefore, which seeks to involve legal profession in the process of social change in the Indian society, would succeed only to the extent to which it is informed by some of its fundamental shortcomings.

CHAPTER FIVE

PROFESSIONAL LEISURE : ITS NATURE AND FUNCTION : SOME SOCIO-SPATIAL SETTINGS AT A DISTRICT COURT BAR

THE STUDY pertains to Gobindgarh District Court (Pseudonym) in Punjab, field work for which was undertaken during 1973-75, alongwith my doctoral research. The data is being presented here for the first time and has not figured earlier in part or full, whether in my book : (Lawyers at a District Court : A Study in the Sociology of Legal Profession, Jawaharlal Nehru University, 1978) or in the book (Lawyers and Touts : A Study in the Sociology of Legal Profession, Hindustan Publishing Corporation, New Delhi, 1982).

We look upon a lawyer's social setting at the court as comprised of the following spatial sub-settings :

(1) His seat.

(2) The bar-room setting, comprised of various enclosures where he may sit in the company of his colleagues while not engaged in any court-room pleading.

(3) The Court-room where he conducts pleading on behalf of his clients.

(4) Physical space in-between the above three settings which he may occupy while shifting between any of the above mentioned three spaces, and where he might have some 'passing' conversation or exchange with clients or colleagues.

(5) The bar library.

We may mention at the outset that the above-mentioned five sub-settings constitute the whole range of professional *situation* lived by a lawyer at Gobindgarh courts. Alternatively, these could also be described as five *social spaces* occupied by him while at the district courts in the discharge of his professional role.

In this chapter, our concern will be with No. (2) of the above mentioned components, i.e. the Bar Room setting. The term 'bar room' sounds a slight misnomer at least in the context of as many as six district courts of Punjab which we happened to visit in addition to the one selected for our study here, since in none of these places did we come across a *single bar room* used by all the lawyers of a court as a sitting room while not engaged in court-work or in giving consultations to the clients. Instead, we found clusters of lawyers occupying different physical spaces in the court's compound more or less regularly. The clusters we came across at Gobindgarh Court were not chancey or random. Instead, they had an enduring character and obtained through regular sitting—behaviour on the part of the bar members. Because of this, they could not be regarded merely as 'amorphous collectivities', but instead, *seemed* to have some attributes of a group or a quasi-group. We thus choose to call them *Interaction Sets*, i.e. sets of individuals engaged in some enduring interaction. In all the district courts that we visited, we found that *bar library building* provided a physical nucleus to these sets, so that even in Gobindgarh court, all but one of these clusters were located around this structure. At the Gobindgarh District Court, there were as many as four interaction-sets, three around the bar room library building and one apart in the farther corner of the court-compound. We shall designate these as A, B, C and D, and analyse them together under certain theoretical categories. Our particular concern will be to view and analyse the nature of social-professional activity associated with these interaction sets.

A note on the methodology of observation may be in order here. The researchers's acquaintance with and acceptance by various bar-room clusters was a gradual process and took 2-3 months. It was at these clusters that I fixed up appointments with various bar-members and also got introduced to new sets of respondents for much of my doctoral research. I was accepted un-suspectingly by the various members of the clusters like a regular 'peripheral' who did not participate in the discussions, but only sat and observed. I sat for hours—on end and watched cluster—members shift between the court-room and the cluster-setting. Rarely did I venture to give my opinion on any topic being discussed there, or sought an information. These clusters served as excellent observation—posts on the professional on-goings, connecting me, at the same time more and more with the bar-members.

(A) COMPOSITION

We shall view the composition of these sets in terms of the following constituents :

(i) Location and Historicity

Three of the four sets i.e. B, C and D, comprising mostly of the lawyers practising on the civil side, were placed around the bar library building, and the fourth i.e. A, comprising mostly of practitioners on the criminal side, was located apart from these three and was placed close to the main gate of the Court's Compound. Two of these sets i.e. A and B had well-built enclosures with barbed overhead ceilings of corrugated sheets along with fan-fittings. The remaining two were located in the open lawns on the three flanks of the library building, their road-side fringes being enclosed with barbed wires. In addition to these clusters, adjacent to the enclosure A, there was an old bar room, rarely used now by the lawyers. However, one did come across some occasional lawyers sitting there with their clients. Tradition goes that this bar room was earlier occupied exclusively by Britain-trained barrister or bar-at-laws. As an eighty-five years old non-practising barrister, reported :

> ......I can tell you how it was in the year 1912 when I came to practise here for the first time. This bar room was exclusively reserved for barristers who practised without exception on the criminal side. We sat, gossiped and drank by ourselves without a member from the rest of the bar ever joining us. Sometimes the Collector would come and join us during lunch time, asking his orderly to bring his bottle of drink to the bar

room......The rest of the bar members thought of us as elites and often said that we were snobs.

As the time passed, more and more non-barristers came to join criminal practice. As a result, this bar room came to be frequented more or less by all criminal lawyers. As for the other enclosures, it was reported that civil and revenue lawyers had started sitting there in small clusters around the library building roughly forty years back. Subsequently, only two of these clusters endured and came to be formalized as distinct clusters i.e. B and D. The last of the four sets i.e. D was barely a decade old and was located in a vast enclosure on the outer flank of the library building in the direction of the main gate of the Courts. In the late-afternoons, however, some younger bar-members could be seen playing badminton in this space, in the company of the bar-president. Another indication of the yet-fluid character of this cluster was provided by the fact that some younger members of the nearby District Income Tax Bar who had started visiting Gobindgarh courts in search of some civil business could be seen sitting in a batch of 3-4 in one corner of this open enclosure. Another distinctive feature of this enclosure was that the lawyers sitting here received their clients within the enclosure itself whereas in nearly all the other enclosures, lawyers left their enclosures to talk to their visiting clients or other acquaintances. We may infer from this that as an interaction-set at the Gobindgarh Courts grew older and older, it developed a more 'exclusive' professional character in the sense that it came to be frequented only by the lawyers to the exclusion of their clients. So, unlike other enclosures, this enclosure did not have the distinctive and exclusive character.

(ii) Social Composition

As remarked above, each of the interaction-sets was characterised by more or less enduring membership. There was in each case, what may be called the *core-membership* and also the *peripheral membership*. The former were those who sat in their own sets regularly and daily. They rarely, if at all, went to spend-time in sets other than their own. On the other hand, peripheral members would shuttle between two or more interaction-sets in a day but still spent more than three-fourth of their off-the-court room time in any one set as against the other sets. There were peripheral in another sense also, i.e. they did not play an active role in the discussions at the interaction-sets ; instead they merely listened without giving any opinion on any issue except that they sometime smiled and nodded their assent to a viewpoint being expressed by one member or another. Also, it was an extremely rare thing to see a peripheral member initiating a discussion or introducing a topic for discussion.

The approximate numerical composition of the *core* as well as peripheral membership of the four sets was as follows :

TABLE : *Core and Peripheral Membership of Interaction Sets*

S. No.	*Interaction Set*	*Core Membership*	*Peripheral Membership*
1.	A	45	13
2.	B	25	11
3.	C	15	6
4.	D	4	7

TABLE : *Caste Composition of Core Membership in the Interaction Sets*

S. No.	*Caste*	*Sets*				*Total membership in the sets*	*Total membership in the bar*
		A	B	C	D		
1.	Jatsikh	23	4	—	—	27	31
2.	Khatri	14	8	5	—	27	63
3.	Arora	1	5	5	1	12	23
4.	Brahmin	5	4	—	3	12	23
5.	Bania	—	3	5	—	8	11
6.	Christian	1	—	—	—	1	1
7.	Goldsmith	1	—	—	—	1	3
8.	Ahluwalia	—	1	—	—	1	3
Total		45	25	15	4	89	154

Note the following observations on the above table :

1. No single caste is as heavily represented in any of the interaction sets as Jatsikhs in set A (66% of its total membership)
2. Besides, this caste is represented only in one more set i.e. B where it constitutes less than one-sixth of its total membership.
3. Of all the four more numerical castes represented in the above table, Jatsikhs have their largest proportion participating as core-members in these sets.

As is obvious, 89 or 57 per cent of the total bar membership of 154 was found participating in the interaction-sets with another 26 or 24 per cent as peripherally participative. On the whole then, not more than one-fifth of the bar membership could be regarded as extraneous to the activity in these interaction sets. The above table reports the caste-composition of the core-membership of various interaction sets.

These three observations lead us automatically to the conclusion that in terms of mutual participation (or set-participation) Jatsikhs possess the highest degree of *cohesiveness* or *solidarity*.

(iii) Age-Composition

Following four tables report on the age-composition of lawyers in the interaction-sets under study. The analysis is confined only to their primary or core members.

TABLE : *Age-Composition of Interaction Set A*

S. No.	*Age-Group*	*Frequency*	
		N	%
1.	22—35	12	26.6
2.	36—45	17	37.7
3,	46—55	7	15.5
4.	56—65	9	20.0
Total		45	99.8

TABLE : *Age-Composition of Interaction Set B*

S. No.	*Age-Group*	*Frequency*	
		N	%
1.	35—45	5	20
2.	46—55	5	20
3.	56—65	9	36
4.	66—75	6	24
Total		25	100

TABLE : *Age-Composition of Interaction Set C*

S. No.	*Age-Group*	*Frequency*	
		N	%
1.	55—59	5	33.3
2.	60—64	3	20.0
3.	65+	7	46.6
Total		15	99.9

TABLE : *Age-Composition of Interaction Set D*

S. No.	*6 Age-Group*	*Frequency*	
		N	%
1.	42	1	25
2.	50	1	25
3.	52	1	25
4.	58	1	25
Total		4	100

A comparative study of the above tables reveals that the youngest segment (i.e. 22-35 yrs.) of the 'clustered' bar is confined only to set A, where it constitutes more than one-fourth of the total membership of the set. This is despite the fact that even though most of the set members were practising on the criminal side, a majority of the younger members were doing 'mixed' practice. This set was also distinctive in another sense. Not only did it have the largest segment of those in the youngest age-bracket, but also of those who constituted the middle-age bracket (i.e. 36-45). The only other set where this age-bracket was significantly represented was B, which had roughly half the proportion that A had in this age-range.

Set A was different from all other sets in that it had none of its members younger than 55 years of age. Incidentally, nearly all its members were considered as constituting the top-layer of Gobindgarh bar in civil and revenue practice.

The smallest of the sets was set D which had only four members. Three among these were late-starters in the profession and the fourth one was a local contractor's son having only a peripheral interest in practice. Some of the set-members had had more than twelve years of practice.

(B) INTERACTION

The interaction within these sets was uni-focal, i.e. it was only convivial; lawyers talked and gossiped among themselves sitting within these enclosures and filled vacant spaces of time with conversational interchanges. Rarely did we come across three or more than three lawyers sitting within these enclosures without talking to each other. The conversation could concern any issue or problem, from poetry, mysticism and religion on the one hand to politics, poverty, prostitution, on the other. It could as well be about the sale of free-hold plots or about the career that could best suit one's child after graduation.

These bar-room gossips were completely un-structured and un-scheduled. A member might casually remark about anything which would eventually broaden into a generalized discussion. Or it might initially be a dyadic exchange into which more and more persons were gradually drawn. One might have read a report on any political event or a scandal in the day's newspaper and its reporting in the cluster might be followed by a variety of interpretations by various bar members present in the enclosure. Or, one might report that such and such a magistrate was not as incorruptible as he was made out to be since his own client had confessed having passed on the graft to him. From this the discussion might be lifted to a general plane of corruption of judiciary and of the political life, so on and so forth. Even though, a topic might emerge out of a casual comment, but having once come into being, it continued to stay and occupy the attention and time of the members till the saturation-point was reached, or when the main discussants dispersed simultaneously on being summoned to the Court-room or by the clients.

The conversation in the bar room had an impersonal character and unless all the main discussants dispersed simultaneously and a lull resulted, it went on continuously like a self-propelled flow. On summons from his client or munshi that the case had been called up in the court, a lawyer in the thick of his argument would barely think it necessary to finish the sentence-on-the tongue; instead, one got up suddenly from his seat, and headed for the court. This termination of the conversation which might look sudden and offensive to an outsider, did not look the least so to the participants themselves who soon picked up something else to occupy themselves.

Note the following illustration from conversation between two middle-aged lawyers in the enclosure A.

X "After all there are some principles which even a politician will have to adhere to in order to survive...Otherwise, he will not be elected the next time".

Y "...It is fantastic that even after 25 years of practice you are so innocent and un-realistic...it is public appearance that they have to bother about like the Gandhi-cap, Khadi or the polished shoe, and not what they really do...".

At that point, another middle-aged lawyer "P" puts in "...Yes, yes, I agree with you...don't you know that dog of a leader...the municiple commissioner, who was caught dead drunk with a prostitute and a pot-full opium...I remember having had a good look at that bitch...she was real fire and full of lust...I don't know if even a magistrate would find it possible to resist her...".

Y "...Yes, I know, you would even abstain from Sessions in order to be with her".

X "...No, he won't do that...he would take her along to the Sessions...because he won't trust that any of his brother-lawyer would not lay her meanwhile."

Caustic wit, banter and repartee were found to be the hallmarks of these conversations. Boredom was rare and the stillness in the atmosphere was often relieved even with vulgarized sexual expressions. One might narrate with cool detachment from the case one had handled earlier, the act of forced coitus with all the ebb and flow of the situation in which woman was invariably made out to be a willing accomplice. But vulgarised, pornographic expressions were invariably related to the person or the situation being described and never to any of the colleagues in bar, except in joke.

These bar-room conversations were *egalitarian* in character. Any one of the members present may initiate the discussion and all may participate in it from across the barrier of caste, age, practice-type or professional status. Despite a comprehensive mapping of the conversational interaction observed within these sets, we found no evidence on the pre-eminence of any of the socio-professional denominators mentioned in the preceding. Conviviality and easy comraderie was manifest at any point of discussions or interchanges. In none of the hundred-odd discussion-sessions attended in these sets did we find the line of consensus on a topic of discussion, drawn essentially along caste-lines.

We now proceed to note some of the interactional peculiarities of various sets. This we shall do both in terms of *intensity* of interaction as well as *contents* of the interaction. Of all the sets, A looked most interactive. As already noted this set was markedly distinctive in that its members spent *much larger chunks of their off-the-court time* in this set than members of any other set did in their respective sets. It is true at least in the case of three-fourth of its members that the only place where they spent time besides court-room and their own seats, was in their enclosure, exception being made for their lunch-time absence when they were seen dining at the only available canteen close to enclosure for set B. The remaining one-fourth members of set A who frequented other sets besides their own were mostly the younger members of the bar with one-to-five years of practice regularity. This, to their credit and *exclusiveness* of presence at the enclosure was not found in other sets, most of whose members frequented one or more of the other sets besides their own even though for a short while. But on the whole, it would be a safe generalization that nearly all the set members of A, B, C and D visited, besides their own set, set or sets of the same practice classification i.e. *civil* or *criminal* as the case may be.

Another indicator of the relative cohesiveness of set A was the convention of tea-sharing among its members which was nearly non-existent in other sets. For this interactional peculiarity of this set, the younger members of this set were responsible. There was a remarkable conviviality among them which found expression in the celebration of small happy episodes in their day-to-day life. One might have come to the Court in a new outfit or might have just received a hundred rupee note from his client—and his friends may force him to celebrate it by 'calling tea'. Or, the occasion might be a member's engagement or his opening an independent office somewhere in the city. Such persuasions for ordering tea were more often succumbed to than resisted or turned down. Of course, some trivial persuasions such as 'you should call for tea since you are looking very smart today' or 'you look like getting a good client soon enough' or 'you should celebrate getting that charming lady as your client' were simply laughed away. Besides these young lawyers, the only other person who was observed throwing tea-parties in this set was the bar president* who every now and then ordered tea on his own and served the set-members.

All this need not suggest that lawyers in other enclosures did not take tea. In fact, most of the enclosure-members consumed several cups of tea during the day, but in most of the cases, each one was found paying for oneself. Sometimes, indeed when these lawyers were visited by some friends from outside or a potential client, tout or some other connection, tea was called for. In the process, however, the lawyers' colleagues sitting along with them at that time also, sometimes shared a cup or two. But as among the lawyers themselves tea was very infrequently offered or accepted in the interaction sets B, C and D.

Content of Interaction

Interaction sets also seemed to differ from each other distinctly in terms of the content of convivial exchanges in these collectivities. Over one hundred hours spent in these enclosures yielded interesting patterns on the nature and composition of gossips in sets

* The same Mr. Himmat Singh, who is described in the chapter : Election of the Bar President, in the book.

TABLE : *Issues and Topics Discussed at Interaction Sets*

Descending Rank Order	*Topics Discussed in Set (A)*	*Topics Discussed in Set (B)*	*Topics Discussed in Set (C)*	*Topics Discussed in Set (D)*
I.	*Civic and Municiple Affairs* such as local elections, political protests and demonstrations etc.	*Contemporay Politics*; corruption in the government and wider society, decline of professional morality among judges etc.	*Law Discussions*; mostly, mere mention of some recent rulings and legislations from Civil and Revenue side.	*Contemporary Politics*; decline of morals in politics and social life.
II.	*Light and Entertaining Gossips* concerning sex, rape, felony, sodomy.	*Property Talk* : Sale and purchase of property in the city; high rate of property tax and other taxes; building housing colonies etc.	*Court Calender* : Ill distribution of court work over the week days, difficulties in adjusting work at various courts, experienced by the set members, accusations of favouratism on the various judges for accommodating some bar members at the cost of others.	*Professional Morals* : Open acceptance of corruption among lawyers and judges, professional rise possible only through un-professional means, corruption among younger bar members.
III.	*Gossip concerning Local Judiciary and Police*, e.g. lack of professional competence among jud-	*Nostalgic Past*, high integrity and morality among old administrative officials, especially the British offici-	*Character assassinations* of some judges of the Gobindgarh Courts, members of the bar also; unfair	*Career Talk*, their reasons for joining the legal profession and their past experience; excellence of their past

	ges at Gobindgarh, corruption among them and the police.	als; low and cheap prices of necessities as contrasted with spiralling prices in the present times; availability of pure and clean eatables in the past.	manipulations by the bar members at the bar electi-ons.	work-experience contrasted with the banality of legal profession in the contempo-rary days.
IV.	*Criticism of Civil Coll-eagues*; their vanity; fra-udulent practices such as forging a receipt; their pompish manners and their uncharitable opinion of criminal practice and lawyers.	*Poetry and Religion*; includ-ing discussion of urdu poe-try, some religious cults such as *sufism*, *tantrism* etc.		*Family talk*; mention of burdensome family commit-ments; career of children, marriage of daughters; diffi-culty of meeting their com-mitments by pursuing professional ethics.

A, B, C and D. We prepared inventories of topics discussed at each of the sessions that we shared with the lawyers. In the table which follows we have arranged broad issues and topics discussed and gossiped at all the sets. For doing so, we have picked up first four categories of topics in their descending order of preponderance in the discussions.

Even a casual glance at the above table reveals, that the interactional contents of set A are most 'recreative' or entertaining of all. The lawyers under this set were found to have slightly *bohemian* outlook on life, talking mostly on the lighter side of their immediate environs—both professional and social, and rarely touched upon the more serious issues and problems with socio-political bearings and even some of the professional conflicts and problems as reported by some bar members in the other sets. The only profession-related gossip they engaged in, was the criticism of their colleagues in civil practice. This seemed to be a reaction against their "negative" evaluation by their civil colleagues who expressed openly that criminal lawyers did not have to work hard on their cases like the civil lawyers and that they worked in collusion with police officials, judges and touts—which was un-professional. But even this variety of gossip occupies the least important position among the first four gossip-topics. We may, therefore, say that the predominant complexion of gossip in this set was found to be relaxed and jovial nearly every time, the investigator visited the enclosure and spent some time there.

As far as set B is concerned, there is no gossip which may be regarded as 'professional', whether directly or indirectly and in this it is different from all other sets. As the categories of topics listed under this set show, members usually occupy themselves in gossips on general politics, their nostalgic past, aesthetics and property matters. The last two of the four categories make this set appear *retreatist* in their general outlook on life. Even the 'contemporary politics' could be bracketed with these two since it involved discussions on general and macro political problems, far removed from their immediate professional and socio-economic existence. On analysing the discussion patterns a little more closely for this set, we found that 'property' gossip was engaged in mostly and quite regularly, by the senior-most members of this set who on account of age had come down substantially in their practice and were eager to invest and re-invest their financial resources earned during their long career.

On the whole, there were much longer spells of silence between various gossip-sessions in set C than in any other set. Gossip was intermittant and characteristically less involving than in other sets and at times a little dull and ponderous. Also, hardly any controversial exchanges were observed, let alone any heated discussions. The members talked mostly in murmurs and whispers. There was a complete lack of joviality or repartee and both the listeners and the speakers put up a drab and cynical expression. Even though, two of the three listed topics concerned legal profession, on a closer scrutiny they revealed their peripheral character. Court-calender occupied a rather insignificant place in their discussions. The attributes of conversational exchange in this set are to be understood in the light of the fact that a vast majority of core-members of this set were in the last and retreatist phase of their career. They were aged ex-elites of the bar and on the verge of retirement and oblivion from the active phase of their professional life.

Even though the smallest of all the sets with a core-membership of four members, set D, reflects an active concern with the decline of professional morality, these lawyers had a sense of 'lagging behind others' who even though much younger in age had developed ample practice. They maintained that honesty in profession never availed much and it was possible to rise professionally only through touts and alliances with police officials. These lawyers were full of stories and episodes regarding all the bar members occupying top ranks, how they had cheated X or Y through forgery or impersonation, blackmailing and various other frauds.

A 52 years old member of this set who had retired from Military Accounts Department, went on thus :

> "...I have no ambitions like those who tear at the flesh of clients young or old, rich or poor...I get some pension and also manage to earn a bit here...but, no body can

> blame that I have fleeced a client or cheated a colleague. There is a certain level of morality that has already entered into my make-up. I cannot fall from this without feeling wretched. But that should not give you any suggestion that I am in any way less competent. It is only my inability to succumb to corruption that restricts my earnings at the bar to the present level."

Most of the biographical accounts of these lawyers were corroborated by members of other sets. Three of them were fairly late-starters in practice, having spent two or three decades in other careers. They had entered legal profession either on retirement from earlier jobs or after resigning them. That is why, they had a natural urge of unloading themselves of their career and family-problems. Another interesting feature revealed about the gossip in this set was that even though the members were critical of the top-layer of the bar for exploiting the younger bar members, they were equally critical of the youngsters for their un-professional conduct, the casualness with which they would bribe the judges and police officials.

From the above scrutiny of *intensity* as well as *content* of interaction in various sets we may say, at least, this much that their distinctive character is explainable substantially in terms of the professional situation of the members, the type of their practice, the level of their professional attainment, their professional problems and the resulting sense of relative ease or deprivation etc. As for the comparatively greater intensity and informality of interaction among members of criminal set evidenced, through the practice of tea-sharing; and also for the relatively greater degree of cohesiveness evidenced, by the fact of spatial exclusiveness of the set, we might afford an explanation rooted in the very differential structure of civil and criminal practice. Almost every civil case has two or more individuals confronting each other on the adversary positions. These two are respectively represented by at least two counsels on the opposite sides. As against this, on every criminal case, one of the two contending parties is the *State* or the *Government* which is represented by its salaried prosecutor, who is not a member of the bar. Even on some criminal cases where the aggrieved parties engage a lawyer from the bar to assist the public prosecutor, the latter and not the former leads the proceedings on the case. All this affords substantially lesser opportunities for mutual confrontation among the criminal practitioners. Greater conviviality and informality among them is thus, an expression of this very existential condition of their practice.

(C) NORMS

What are some of the expressed or un-expressed norms that guide the interaction in these sets ? It may be said at the very outset that the sets under examination here are not as formalised as groups and as such these do not have norms of interaction in an explicit manner. But even then, since both the membership and interaction in these sets does have an enduring character, it is of necessity that it is 'regulated' and maintained by certain norms—even though these may never be expressed formally by any member. By a regular observation of interaction in various sets, over a number of sittings, we inferred following norms which constitute the backbone of these interactional exchanges. That these norms are vital for the existence of sets, became obvious especially during situation when these were violated. The members regretted such violations and expressed disapproval of such behaviour. The norms in question are as follows :

(i) Informality

The exchanges are informal and un-structured. Any topic may come up for gossip or discussion. Further, gossip on an issue may remain confined to two or three persons whereas gossip on another issue may charge the whole of the set leading to participation by all the members present at the time. Like its beginning these exchanges also have an informal ending. A member while engaged in a conversation may effect a sudden withdrawal from it on receiving information from his munshi or client to make his appearance in a court on a case. He says nothing by way of 'summing up' or 'apologising' for sudden withdrawal. Others also seem to take this sudden termination in their stride without taking any offence. The topic may thus die out on the departure of a member, without any one else bothering to pick up the lead.

(ii) **Egalitarianism**

No distinction is made between members with a high or low professional status or in terms of their caste, creed or age etc. in so far as the interaction is concerned. Any one of the members may participate in a discussion when it becomes a generalized exchange without surprising any body. Also, none is discouraged by any other member from stating his opinion, un-expectedly. There were rare instances of a member being interrupted in the middle of his statement. It was often observed that a gossip started with comments by one of the senior-most members of the bar and closed with comments by a junior member.

(iii) **No Personalised Gossip**

It was very rare that the members resorted to personal invective or slander against each other while gossiping in the sets. Nor was there any occurrence of slander, villification or even mention of clients or contacts of colleagues from within the same set. There was of course, some observations on slanderous talking about colleagues in the other sets. Also, members rarely exchanged any personal details about their practice, family or other intimate affairs. Lot of fun was drawn from person-centered gossips about-colleagues in other sets. In a few cases which were observed of members talking about themselves or their family affairs, the listeners or on-lookers posed no curious questions or queries and listened to the speaker with an abject expressionless. No body provided matching details from one's own personal life or experience to continue the conversation, and this brought the end of such gossip, rather too soon.

(D) FUNCTION

From the preceding account the question comes up: what is the function of these sets ? What do they contribute to the lawyers' professional routine and also to the bar as a whole ? What would have happened in the absence of these sets ?

(i) Role-Synchronic

The interaction sets are *role-synchronic* in the sense that they bring together or synchronise various social components of lawyers' role. These components are *lawyers*, *clients* and *munshis*—which may respectively be regarded as role-actors, role-alters and role-subordinates. By their very physical placement in the courts' compound and their accessibility to both munshis and clients, the sets co-ordinate these constituents with the primary role-actors—the lawyers. Both the munshis and clients come to inform the lawyers at these enclosures that the case has been called up and that their presence was required in the court because of ready availability here. The absence of these interaction sets where the said information is conveyed, calls for some *functional equivalent* which links the lawyers to the courts, and also which links their professionally—'passive' moments to those of professional activity.

These enclosures were also found serving as contact-points for clients who came to see their lawyers in order to know the progress on their cases. They would come looking for their lawyers only to the particular enclosures where the lawyers were known to sit usually. Some shy clients would keep standing on the periphery of these enclosures, trying to catch the glance of their counsels. Having noticed the clients, the counsel concerned would leave his seat and come to the client standing outside the enclosure, apprise him of the situation on his case or give whatever consultation he wanted to, and then get back to the enclosure. We observed that lawyer handling revenue or criminal cases were visited for such consultations much more than those handling civil cases. Further, most of these clients were drawn from rural nexus. These lawyer-client consultations which are occasioned on account of the ready availability of lawyers at their interaction-sets may also be subsumed under the role-synchronic function of the sets since this provides a continuity to their practice by perpetuating a particular business-transaction between the lawyer and his client.

(ii) Cathartic Function

As the analysis of the contents of interaction exchange shows, there was no serious-minded professional exchange at these sets.

Most of the groups were of casual, entertaining type which seem to *perform nothing* but a cathartic function. Whether the professionals suffer from any professional tension generated out of role-conflict, role-ambivalence etc. or not, the fact remains that most of the interactional exchange at the sets has a predominantly *cathartic* complexion. Further, as the table reveals, the set of criminal lawyers has a stronger cathartic complexion than the other three sets. This may be understood as a consequence of larger incidence of unprofessional practices in criminal practice than in civil practice.

(iii) **Profession-Cohesive**

The exchanges in these interaction sets do seem to perform a certain 'cohesive' function. This is not to say that the lawyers representing two adversary clients will not face each other in the court-room with the characteristic ferocity associated with a lawyer's role, simply because they both belong to the same interaction. All the same the casual, fraternal off-beat exchanges between them in these sets, do seem to remove or moderate any poignancy that may have resulted from any exchanges in the court-room. Such a significance was attributed to them by some respondents when called upon to comment :

> "This is just like sitting on the village chaupal (common meeting place), or like sitting on the river-bank with your clothes off before taking the dip......at least it keeps your monotony away while you don't have anything else to do......"

Some Theoretial Considerations

Finally, we shall reflect on the theoretical question : what is the theoretical nature of the convivial exchange which goes on in various sets ?

How should we classify the interactional activity ? Does it correspond to 'work' or 'leisure' or both ? Before we answer this question, let us first understand : What is leisure ?

Sociologists (e.g. Dumazedier, 1968) engaged in the study of leisure do admit that leisure in the sense of 'respite from work' has always been present in all human societies where it was found mixed up inextricably with leisure and it was difficult to tell one from the other.[1] Nevertheless, the true genre of leisure according to them came to be evolved only in the modern industrial societies, because it is here that leisure is marked by its two *essential* characteristics. First, it is only in such societies that day-to-day activities are not governed by certain common ritual obligations as in the case of tribal or pre-industrial societies. Second, it is only in these societies that work is sharply separated from other activities. Accordingly, one of the recent sociologists of leisure ascribes three essential attributes to this modern variety of leisure.[2]

(*i*) It is free from any obligation. It represents freedom both from any gainful employment as well as from other social institutional obligations. Thus, all the off-work time is 'free' time. But 'leisure time' is only one constituent of it, since much of 'free' time or off-work time is also used to discharge many physical, or other Jobs. Social 'leisure' time corresponds to net free time available after discharging these multifarious commitments.

(*ii*) It is 'dis-interested' in that it is not governed by any pecuniary, commercial or utilitarian motives.

(*iii*) It is a diversion sought as an end in itself for the self-satisfaction of the seeker.

Let us have a look at the interaction of our study in the light of above said three attributes of leisure.

Lawyers' sitting in the sets and their being engaged in convivial exchange as such does not constitute a gainful activity. They do not make money merely by sitting there and by chit-chating. But, all the same, their sitting here does come within the overall framework of their gainful activity and also it does perform a co-ordinating and integrating function towards it. So, even though the lawyers do not charge anything from their clients while sitting in these

1. Jaffree Dumazedier "Leisure" in *International Encyclopaedia of Social Sciences*, Vol. 9, McMillan Co. and The Free Press, 1968, pp. 248-254.

2. *Ibid.*

enclosures, they do promote and perpetuate their chances of being paid by their clients through their presence here.

As for its 'freedom from obligation' interactional exchange under study, here does apparently correspond to this ideal-typical stipulation. But, there is something more than meets the eye, since 'sitting in the bar' rather than on one's seat or elsewhere is an established professional practice and continues as a part and parcel of the professional tradition; therefore, lawyers' presence in the bar enclosures is not entirely a free activity. It is in obligation to the tradition of legal profession.

As for the last two characteristics, we might say that there is very little correspondence between the two situations. The element of 'deliberate choice' which is reflected in both these characteristics is absent in the activity under examination. The lawyers do not pursue it consciously or purposively and also they are not conscious of some benefit to their personality out of this activity. Rather it comes as a consequence of the cathartic contents of the interactional exchange', we are tempted to grant a 'diversionary' character to it. Thus, eventhough it is a diversion, it is not a 'sought out diversion for the good of the personality'. Rather, it is an un-intended outcome of a certain institutionalized professional tradition or practice.

In summing up, therefore, we might say that even though the interactional exchange under study does have a cathartic content and composition, and thus come close to the 'diversionary' character of leisure, it does not satisfy the most basic prerequisite of leisure, i.e. of being defined sharply as a component of off-work or 'free' time. Rather being located as it is within the overall framework of work, the interaction under consideration seems closer to the primitive or non-industrial genre-of leisure where both work and play are inter-meshed imperceptibly. This seems quite significant in view of the fact that the legal profession, whose component the 'leisure' under consideration here is, belongs more particularly to the modern industrial times. The 'purity' or the 'mixed' nature of leisure, therefore, need not be coterminous with the modern-industrial or primitive societies as often maintained by sociologists of leisure.

CHAPTER SIX

POTENTIALS AND PARAMETERS OF SOCIAL CHANGE THROUGH LAW IN CONTEMPORARY INDIAN SOCIETY : A SOCIOLOGICAL ASSESSMENT

THE PRESENT CHAPTER is a synoptic view of the problem of *Social Change Through Law in India,* in some of its restricted dimensions only. The question to which we have tried to address ourselves is : whether or not it is possible to carry out the process of social change—as per some of the socially accepted goals and objectives, through the instrumentality of law ? While the search for parameters on which the facilitation of change through law depends may seem interminable, our focus here will be only on some of the intra-systemic parameters, i.e. such aspects or features as relate to the legal system itself. This choice is purely heuristic and notwithstanding the fact that the ecology of change is integral and embraces the legal system and its institutions, as well as several other sub-systems such as economic, cultural, political and even symbolic. This chapter is divided into three sections : career of western law and legal system in India; institutional setting; legal profession and its contemporary orientations. Later, we shall draw inferences from these three sections in our attempt to answer the question : what are the potentialities of social change through law in contemporary Indian society ?

CAREER OF WESTERN LAW AND LEGAL SYSTEM IN INDIA : THE HISTORICITY AND MODERNITY

The historicity of a legal system is of paramount significance. It defines the parameters of the role that it can possibly play in the process of social change. Accordingly, it may either facilitate or accelerate law's intended participation in the achievement of certain social goals or it may constrict or even obviate its intended objective of facilitating a change in the social reality, and instead provide a smoke-screen behind which the forces of *status quo* continue to operate and perpetuate the pre-existent structures of inequity and deprivation.

In India, modern law and its allied institutions based upon the legitimacy of rational-legality were never created with a view to achieve any explicit social goals adopted by the collective will or consensus of the Indian people. Instead, these were founded, refined and elaborated by the British colonial masters purely with the purposes of strengthening their political-administrative hold over the colony. They sought to devise and formulate such codifications with which they could address themselves equally to ethnically diverse sets of population. Thus, as the *Pax Britannica* was extended to increasingly larger reaches of territory and population, law was elaborated both in its *procedural* as well as *substantive* aspects. Lindsay[1] sums up this process of codification as follows :

> The first Indian Law Commission, under the presidency of Lord Macaulay, was set up in 1934; its most notable achievement was the production of the draft of the Indian Penal Code, which however, did not become law until 1860. Macaulay's Commission also drew up a number of reports which fell under the consideration of succession of Law Commissions, which sat in England at various times between 1853 and 1870 and whose efforts led to the enactment of the Codes of Procedure, civil and criminal, in 1859 and 1861 respectively. This judicial system in India by the amalgamation of the Supreme and *Sadar* Courts into High Courts. This latter fruit of the labour of these commissions were the Succession Act (1865), the Limitation Act (1871), the Evidence Act and

1. Sir, B. Lindsay, 'Law' in LSS O'Mailley : *Modern India and the West*, London, Oxford University Press, pp. 567-581.

the Contract Act (1872), and still later, under the direction of the Government of India, there came the Specific Relief Act (1882) and the Easement Act (1882). By this time, it may be said, the process of codification came to an end, though further legislation of a comprehensive character was undertaken to define the law of land tenure and for the various provisions.

The process of codification continued through the Native Marriages Act in 1872, 'in 1891 a controversial Age of Consent Act was passed. It was further modified in 1929. The Press Act came into being in 1879, News Paper Act in 1908; the Factory Act was passed, in 1881; in 1904 a Co-operative Act was legislated' (Singh).[2] But such an administrative steam-roller broke up the indigenous character of the Indian legal system, which was characterized by autonomy of the customary and the caste law at the rural level and the kingly law—mostly based upon the traditional Hindu and Muslim scriptures, at the level of towns and cities which were the seats of political authority occupied by kings and *rajas*. British courts now, provided alternative juridical authority invokable by one who had even lost his case at the village panchayat or the caste panchayat. Thus, traditional social and caste rivalries which were earlier contained under the necessity of maintaining social harmony, consensus or compromise, were now thrown into the open and found for themselves a new playground in the British law courts. Rural people who had earlier been used to respect the local justice, welcomed the idea of giving their luck another try at the British courts. Thus, justice was perceived as both 'capricious' and 'manipulable' (Cohn).[3] Slowly, but surely, sociologically speaking, all this inhered a basic and fundamental change in the social relations. It was a movement from *status* to *contract*, where the *individual* was abstracted from his socio-cultural milieu and viewed as an entity *equal before law*,

2. Yogendra Singh, 'Legal System, Legitimation and Social Change' in his *Essays on Modernization in India*, Manohar, 1978, p. 146.
3. B. Cohn, "Law and Change in North India", *Economic Development and Cultural Change*, VIII, I, 1959, pp. 79-93.

to another of the same kind. Corporate rights and responsibilities were thus, replaced by individual ones (Galanter).[4] It also meant a shift from holistic perspective of justice, when an issue was related to its antecedents, to a partial and fragmented perspective when a single issue was focussed upon and judged in abstraction from its background, purely in terms of the principle of logic and consistency.[5]

But even though this 'impersonal' and 'alien' character of the British law was against the socio-cultural genius and needs of the Indian people, it has continued to stay and thrive having once been established. Two main reasons were mainly responsible for this. Firstly, the increasing political consolidation of the British over India lent increasing legitimacy to their *rule of law* and gave it almost an honorific character in the perception of the Indian people. Secondly, the entrenchment of the rule of law along with the Indianization of the British bureaucracy in India, created an elitist class constitutive of both lawyers and administrators, entirely dependent upon and interested in the perpetuation of the legal system. The system came to acquire further legitimacy through the entire life of the Indian freedom movement, which was spearheaded by lawyers who used with effective advantage their knowledge of *law* and *legality*. The majority of these leaders such as Mahatma Gandhi, Motilal Nehru, Jawaharlal Nehru, Tilak, Bholabhai Desai and others were trained lawyers and barristers who profited immensely from their grounding in law both to create a sense of political awareness among the people as well as to weaken the legitimacy of British rule in India. Subsequently, some of these law-trained people like Jawaharlal Nehru, Patel, Ambedkar

---

4. Marc Galanter, "The Modernization of Law" in M. Weiner (ed.), Modernization : The Dynamics of Growth, London, Basic Books, 1966.
5. This consequence was positively dysfunctional for the overall social order, in as much as all those conflicts which were either sorted out earlier on account of social pressures towards consensus or were subdued through similar reasons, now became manifest and at times virulent. All this cut into the very foundation of the once-effective *Panchayats*—the grass roots level of justice and also started weakening the resilience of the joint family system. (See J.S. Gandhi, *Lawyers and Touts : A Study in the Sociology of Legal Profession*, Hindustan Publishing Corporation, New Delhi, 1982).

also played a pivotal role in the making of the Indian Constitution after independence in 1947. The entire structure of the Constitution bears ample testimony to the *legalistic-formalistic* cognition of the Indian reality, on the part of its framers. The highly idealistic and euphoric tone in which some of its provisions are cast betokens the characteristic optimism which lawyers would naturally have in the capacity of law to change the existing social reality.

Note, for example, the provision regarding the abolition of Untouchability under Art. 17 : ' "Untouchability" is abolished and its practice in any form is forbidden. The enforcing of any disability arising out of "Untouchability" shall be an offence punishable in accordance with law'. Or, for that matter note the preamble to the Constitution :

> The people of India, having solemnly resolved to constitute India into a SOVEREIGN DEMOCRATIC REPUBLIC and to secure to all its citizens : JUSTICE, Social, economic and political ; LIBERTY of thought, expression, belief, faith and worship ; EQUALITY of status and of opportunity ; and to promote among them all FRATERNITY assuring the dignity of the individual and the unity of the Nation;...

The text of the Constitution, however, does not provide the corresponding strengths to the citizens in the realization of the above mentioned utopian objectives. This is obvious from the fact that whereas all the *Fundamental Rights* (viz., rights to equality before law; right to freedom of expression; of religion, of association; right to hold property, etc.) as listed under Articles 19-35 are guaranteed through *justiciability, Directive Principles of State Policy* (Articles : 36-51) which relate to such provisions as individuals' right to adequate means of livelihood, equal pay for equal work, protection of youth and childhood against exploitation, securing of living wage to industrial and agricultural workers etc. are *non-justiciable.* It is enjoined upon the state, however, to move in the direction that the objectives listed under the Directive Principles of State Policy are achieved, without providing any specific legal sanction against the government which does not do so. It seems indeed a patent attempt—advertant or inadevertant, at mystifying the long-established institutions of inequity and deprivation (illustrated ideally in the institution of caste). This is so because there is no leverage provided against any such political lobbying which may bend the state apparatus to its own advantage and thereby hold in perpetual abeyance the realization of these objectives. Once again, therefore, we have evidence of a *formalistic* mentality, which through inadequate appreciation of socio-political and economic complexity, reifies the mere form of law into a strong bulwark of peoples' protection against inequity and discrimination. The Constitution is a unique caricature of a futile hope which conveniently forgets that structurally given and traditionally legitimized inequities are potent enough to frustrate the realization of even the most clearly intended codifications. Baxi[6] (1982, p. 7) copiously illustrates with what scant regard the law and legalism are treated both by the ruler and the ruled. He says :

> Most people regard legal rules as irritating, more costly or unavailable. This generates a demonstration effect. If people who are at the helm of affairs or are rich, resourceful or affluent, do not follow rules when these adversely affect their interests, other people who have to follow rules are likely to do so, not because the rules themselves are justified or legitimate but because they are powerless. They follow rules which hurt their self-interests, because they have no choice.

In the popular perception the breach of law, rather than its adherence is legitimized : '...all this (i.e. the easy exploitability of law) has the effect of convincing a large segment of the Indian people that rule-following is not *merely unjustified* but counter-productive in terms of their interests'.[7] What explains this easy exploitability, manoeuvrability of law or rather, what explains this unbounded faith that people have in the resourcefulness of law to deliver the goods ?

---

6. Upendra Baxi, *Alternatives in Development Law: The Crisis of the Indian Legal System*, (Vikas Publishing House, New Delhi), 1982, p. 7.
7. *Ibid.*, p. 8.

To answer this, we have again to refer to the original, historical compulsions behind the genesis and evolution of the present legal system in India, which was more an administrative necessity than a response to the felt needs of the people. Its character of *impersonality* and *anonymity* did not fit into the *gemeinschaft* character of Indian society, where to exist socially, was to harmonize and consensualize with the social environment rather than seeking the protection of one's 'isolate' interests vis-a-vis the rest of society through hiring legal muscles (advocates) in fighting adversarial court battles.

It needs restatement that the putatively unified western law system which sought the displacement of earlier decentralized and autonomized local juridical structures and sub-structures, did not emerge as a response to a qualitative change in people's expectations from justice, but rather took such a change for granted. Nothing that happened as a result of the spread of colonial administration in India generated such compulsions as to make people *need* different sytsems of justice, i.e. *modern* as against the *traditional* one.[8]

Another point—that can only be conjectured here for want of space, is that in most countries of the world, the growth and evolution of a *modern law* system has accompained the growth of an independent industrial economy, one which grows in response to the needs of the indigenous society. In India, as against this, all through the nineteenth and twentieth centuries till the independence of 1947, the economy had functioned primarily as a captive-economy furthering the interests of colonial economic systems. All this held in check the growth of such commerce, trade and industry as would have created automatic compulsions for a natural proliferation and acceptance of rational legal codification.

8. This is, however, not to say that once the new system came into being, it did not become popular. Rather, what is being said here is that people looked upon this system as an additional theatre in which to pursue once again the fight that they had lost in the traditional system ; also, that the system proved dyfunctional so that it gave a rude blow to the time-tried traditional system of justice to which people had got habituated.

INSTITUTIONAL SETTING

In order to draw cogent inferences on the effectivity of the legal system in ushering the process of social change, one must examine the functional health of the overall system of justice and law-making in the country. This could include examining in detail the process of law-making and law reform in the country as well as examining courts as working systems in so far as whether or not they fulfil or try to fulfil the constitutionally given goals and objectives. A thorough reading of the Constitution,[9] as well as various policy documents relating to national planning[10] would bring into bold relief the egalitarian-equalitarian ethos which constitutes the most strongly cherished national objective. At the present level of information and awareness, we cannot go into this critical question of compatibility between the said institutional setting and the egalitarian-equalitarian goal. A thorough examination of the structure and functioning of courts within the framework of organizational Sociology and Psychology is likely to yield both diagnostic as well as prescriptive insights regarding the process of law making (i.e. through courts judgments) as well as law reforms. Pending such thorough research into this area, we can evaluate in brief whatever little evidence exists at present.

(i) Higher Judiciary and its Orientation to the Basic Social Goals

When one thinks of the important role to be played in the process of social change, one expects at least due vigilance on their part which would discourage violation of the fundamental rights of the citizenry. As far as the present record of the apex courts is concerned, one finds a display of sheer pusillanimity by the higher judiciary. Some writers on the contemporary legal scene in India, such as Upendra Baxi, a Delhi Law School Professor and, Krishan Mahajan, a *Hindustan Times* law-specialist and others, have cited copious illustrations in support of this contention. Baxi[11] writes :

---

9. Govt. of India, Law and Justice, *The Constitution of India*, 1973, New Delhi.
10. Govt. of India, *The First Five Year Plan—A Draft Outline*, New Delhi, 1957.
11. U. Baxi, *op. cit.*, pp. 210-211.

> In Tamil Nadu, as early as 1961, a prisoner prayed for a *writ of mandamus*, under Article 226 of the Constitution, directing the Superintendent, Central Jail, Trichirappalli, to act in accordance with rules 38, 278, 637, 640, 641, 379, 354, 366 and 651 to 658 of the Tamil Nadu Prisons and Reformatory Manul (Vol. II). His grievance was that the jail was overcrowded, as a result of which he (while serving a sentence of rigorous imprisonment) was not merely deprived of proper accommodation but also of minimum necessities such as 'food', bathing facilities, scavenging facilities, etc.' in gross violation of the above mentioned rules. The High Court dismissed the petition (W.P. No. 1234 of 1961, disposed of on 20 November, 1961) although it conceded that the petitioner's grievance was 'not entirely unfounded' and that it was 'not entirely imaginary or unreal.'

This is only one of several such cases in which the Court buckled under the weight of procedural wrangles and failed to rise in support of constitutionally granted fundamental rights. It will, therefore, be futile to hope that the courts will be ready to play any protective role in the application and interpretation of the state law.

Further, there is a pronounced degree of *ad-hocism* in the day-to-day functioning of the courts. Rise in litigation and the piling arrears have taken a heavy toll of *consistency* in the judgments given by the courts. In a poignant narration, Mahajan[12] illustrates how, for want of internal communication and co-ordination between different benches of the Supreme Court of India, three persons equally convicted for the same crime of murdering a family, met different fates. In the case of one of the co-accused, a death sentence was commuted to life imprisonment; in the second case, the Supreme Court sent the mercy petition to the President for reconsideration; in the third case—that of Jeeta Singh—the death sentence was carried out. Does it not amount to playing with the most fundamental rights, viz. the right to life ? Mahajan maintains that such lack of internal communication between the various

12. Krishan Mahajan, "Weep for Jeeta Singh," *The Hindustan Times*, 16-3-1982.

benches of the Supreme Court does not affect the rich who can pay fat fees to a well informed lawyer as against a poor litigant who through lack of means suffers and rots through default of the courts. He suggests a composite registry-system for the judgments of the various Supreme Court benches, eventually leading to a complete computerization of the judgments.[13] It is a measure of the lack of urge on the part of the country's apex courts to keep in step with the contemporary reality that such dynamic suggestions have been persistently ignored.

(ii) Management of law Reforms

If the social-orientation of the law courts as well as their day-to-day functioning does not inspire us with a positive hope regarding law being able to play a socially relevant role what is the position regarding the process of law reforms ? The loose-jointed *ad-hocism* which we noticed regarding the courts above, seems also to have seeped into the process of law reforms. We shall examine in brief some evidence on this, as presented by Baxi.[14]

The process of law reforms in India is of a highly tentative nature. There is a wide array of bodies, all of them recommendatory in nature, concerned with this process. Before the Law Commission of India came into existence in 1955, one could count a minimum of 39 Working Groups or Law Committees entrusted with the task of law reforming. Even now the Law Commission adheres to this role with several other bodies. There is no specific concept which either overtly or covertly seeks to co-ordinate the law-making recommendations of these bodies.

The Law Commission, whose function is to reform and modify the existing laws and the legal system, is a temporary body and is appointed after every three years. Its functioning as well as composition is marked by a high degree of *ad hocism.* For example, the membership of eight Law Commissions appointed so far, has varied between 4 and 12 and also there has been a substantial time-lag between the appointment of the chairman and the other

13. Krishan Mahajan, "Computerizing Courts", *Ibid.*, 7-7-1982.
14. U. Baxi, *op. cit.*

members. Among its other operative features, it is most important to note that the government enjoys absolute monopoly in the appointment of all the members, including the chairman. This leaves the ruling political powers completely free in staffing the commissions with men of their choice. That they may have substantially succeeded in this, is vivid from the 'virtual absence of dissenting opinions' in the reports submitted by various commissions.

Also, the majority of the commission members have been recruited from the retired judiciary (both of High Courts and Supreme Court). The government has shown no responsiveness whatsoever to the suggestions that the commission membership be also drawn from academic and practising lawyers and from various social sciences such as Psychology, Social work, Sociology etc. The political elites have thus, been able to easily bend an important organ of law reform to their own advantage and interests.

As to the contents of the laws recommended and law reports submitted by various commissions so far, Baxi notes that important social issues and problems such as inequitous agrarian relations, indebtedness and money-lending, tenancy and ceiling reforms, agricultural wages etc. have virtually been untouched. Instead, they have been concerned with taxation law, property law, family law and constitutional amendments—all of which Baxi terms as the *lawyer's law*. There is a correspondence between the above bias on the part of the courts and the bias shown by the government in its treatment of the various law commission reports. Whereas the reports concerning proposed legislations on the procedural law, constitutional amendments and such like matters have been implemented, those dealing with the question of *benami* transactions, married women's property, revision of the Workman's Compensation Act, have so far been shelved.

Whatever little evidence we have considered under this section drives us to the conclusion that as regards some of the fundamental goals of social changes as set out in the Indian Constitution as well as the planning documents, the institutional setting—comprising of both the apex courts as well as the chief law-reforming body—is inappropriately oriented. It shows no dynamism and no capacity to meet challenges of the developing society. The lacuna lies not merely in the inappropriate social orientations, but also—and more fundamentally—in its structure and composition which precluded it from retaining their functional autonomy.

LEGAL PROFESSION AND ITS CONTEMPORARY ORIENTATIONS

(i) Social Unresponsiveness and Mystification

The most important sub-structure of the legal system capable of playing an effective role in the process of social change in any society is comprised of those who use and apply law to day-to-day situations, i.e. lawyers and judges. It is they who draw out the inherent potentials from the existing laws and thus help give rise to new laws through the process of re-interpretation and creation of precedents. They have indeed a very special role to play in a transitional society as India is at present. It is through their efforts that law is related to the newly emergent empirical situations, claims and counter claims, and made increasingly more relevant. What is the existing evidence on the preparedness of these two the categories of personnel to use law in furthering the process of social change, i.e. to help achieve the socially accepted goals of equalitarianism-egalitarianism ? However, we shall focus our attention here only on lawyers, on whom some research-based empirical evidence is possible.

Some researches done at the District court level, i.e. the lowest organizational level of the court hierarchy in India—the other two being High Court and Supreme Court—demonstrate a highly mercenary attitude on the part of the lawyers (Gandhi).[15] They regard their clients as expendable and mere instruments of profit-making and commit all varieties of professional improprieties including bullying, deceit and pressurising, to achieve that. They obviate the very first tenet of professional practice and secure most of their business through touts and mercenaries-using even their lawyer-colleagues as touts, rather than through their professional reputation. Anchored in their intimate familial or caste networks they progress on their way to professional careers. Although

15. J.S. Gandhi, *op. cit.*

specific research evidence on the lawyer practising at High Court and Supreme Court yet remains to be collected, one would expect similar orientations to prevail at these levels too. This is on account of the fundamental and grassroot character of district level professional practice.

The professionals engage themselves in a lot of gimmickry, posing as custodians of the poor and the defenceless, without volunteering to do any service to their cause (1974-75).[16] Numerous Legal Aid Societies and Associations including the National Legal Aid Committee are on record as having engaged themselves in a lot of rhetoric and exhortations about the necessity of providing legal aid to the poor. But they merely want their fees to come from the state instead of private clients.[17] There is no compulsion or persuasion generated by the various professional bodies on the conduct of their members—as has been the case for example in the USA and some other countries, to champion the cause of the poor. This lack of any substantive concern on the part of the lawyers with the endemic problem of poverty, and instead using the AID THE POOR slogan only to generate more work or employment-potential for their own kind, is a poor indicator of the professionals' potentiality to use and apply law in favour of the poor. Despite this poor preparendness for a socially relevant role, the lawyers have high notions about the centrality of their existence in the scheme of things in society. A study into the structure of professional cognitions (1974-75)[18] reveals a complete lack of criticality or reflexivity on their part. They perceive themselves responsible even for the socio-historical causation of the Indian society, cut out to play a crucial role even in its future evolution and development. This involuntary urge at self-mystification unaccompanied by any compe-

16. J.S. Gandhi, "Lawyers and Social Change : A Test Case" *Punjab University Law Review*, XXVII, 1, 2, 1974-75, pp. 46-56.
17. J.S. Gandhi, "Poverty, Profession and Social Change : The role of Legal Profession." paper read at the Fifth National Conference on Social Sciences, New Delhi (January, 1981).
18. *Op. cit.*

tence in terms of their social-orientation, makes them singularly unfit to play any role in furthering the process of social change.

(ii) Growth of Professional Reflexivity

A very noteworthy feature is the growth of socio-professional reflexivity through the medium of non-practising lawyers—especially those engaged in law teaching and journalism. Some highly sensitive and creative thinking has been set in motion by some (even though only a few such as Mahajan, Baxi, S. Sahay etc.) law professors and law columnists. They have touched upon a wide array of issues ranging from critical appraisal of the functioning of the modern legal system and the law courts, the static and unhelpful nature of modern legal codifications and legal procedures to the critical analysis of the practice of law and the needed reforms in the current system of legal education. Some of them have even listed out new roles that the lawyers should take upon themselves to cope with the newly emergent social needs such as participation in public-interest litigation, free legal pleading on behalf of the poor and indigent clients etc. It is through the efforts of such public interest-oriented *lawyers* that some shocking cases of administrative-judicial neglect have been brought into the open. One such incident relates to the recent blinding of undertrials at Bhagalpur Jail by police. Another concerns the callous neglect of the inmates of the institution for the mentally retarded at Agra. Still another relates to the usurpation of traditional earning rights of the poor Chamars (traditionally regarded as untouchables) and Muslims over the carcasses of animals, through the introduction of the system of contract-sales as a result of collusion between the politicians and big business. The Supreme Court was so seized with the lament of poor petitioners that it set up an Investigation Commission, consisting of Baxi and Mahajan, to go into the background of the entire case and report to the court.

A relevant question that needs answering is why this beam of critical reflection on law, legal system and the legal needs of the people has been thrown in by non-practising lawyers rather than by those who earn their livelihood defending their clients in a court of law ? The most obvious reason seems the incapacity of the practising lawyers to detach themselves from the conditions of their practice. Legal practice in Indian society is intensely competitive where many find it difficult even to eke out the barest survival. Another telling feature of professional practice is that it is unaccompanied—at any level of practice, i.e. whether district court, High Court or Supreme Court—by any directions, constraints or persuasions from professional bodies, goading the lawyers to engage themselves in any non-profit activities, such as the defence of the needy and socially rejected. The law-academics or the law-writers like the ones mentioned above, who are exposed to international developments in the sphere of law and its use in society and who find themselves far surpassed in material affluence by even the mediocre practitioners take a plunge into the realm of 'social responsibility' and 'social relevance' with the gusto of a *crusader*. Note the following pungent comments of Mahajan[19] on the inadequacy of the existing system of legal education :

> After 30 years, the Bar Council of India, which controls professional legal education in the country has woken up to the need to include a course on rural laws in the syllabi. Even now under the new five year law course the paper has been kept optional instead of being made compulsory input. This reflects rather poorly on the socio-economic understanding of the advocates and professors who are members of the Council's legal education committee which designs the syllabi.

Or, again, in the same piece, '......How ironic that so much promise should be barren. Can we forgive the law men on the legal education committee who do not even perceive or on perceiving do not nurture the promise. Along with the media men, they have made the law fallow.'

What is the promise of this critical reflexivity spreading among the practising lawyers, creating awareness among them of a new role that they have to play in the contemplated process of

19. Krishan Mahajan, "Making Law Fallow", *The Hindustan Times*, June 8, 1982.

social change ? The prospects for any such transformation in the professional attitude—so vital for effective role-playing in the social change process, are remote and virtually non-existent. There is no conduit via which the intellectual lawyer's sensitivity would be transferred to the perspective of the practising lawyers, who otherwise are under no professional compulsions from their professional and controlling organizations—which if effective, can go to the extent of setting new professional norms for their members. *In sociological terms a new social ethos can be universalized among the members of a collectivity only if they undergo a new, but similar socio-historical experience, or receive a similar orientation under the influence of the same socializing agency.* None of these two posibilities exists in the Indian context. Both sets of professional categories, i.e. socially *sensitive* and *insensitive*, live under two different types of economic conditions and the corresponding normative milieux. There is no possibility, no scope, no pressure whatsoever for inter-swapping of their existential parameters. Hence, the two must live compulsorily as two isolates and under two mutually exclusive preserves. The state can play a conducive role only if it puts at a premium the critical reflexivities and value-orientations of the intellectual lawyers and places them appropriately in certain crucial positions within the apparatus of state planning. But this again is not a foreseable prospect if the state's handling of the Law Commission of India is any guide—from which it has excluded in a studied manner, persons with reflective backgrounds such as law teachers, law writers and social scientists. The plain and obvious conclusion which then one has to reckon with is that there is very little correspondence between values of the political elites and the values of reflexivity, criticality and social relevance represented contemporaneously by the lawyer-intellectual or the socially aware.

THE SUMMING UP

Research materials examined by us in this brief study lead us to negative conclusions as to law's effectivity to facilitate the process of social change in India. There seems little compatibility between the social goals set out by us as a nation or society and the resources and strengths of the legal system to facilitate their achievement. The historically implanted alienative law has become further divorced from the reality of people's lives; it has proliferated without any aspirational thrust from people's lives and its problematics. It is not only the institutional setting of law—both in its composition and functioning which is askewed, but also the orientations of its leading role-players, i.e. the lawyers who are ill-prepared to play any such grandiose role as using law for facilitating the achievement of equalitarian-egalitarian goals. A small sector of the profession, viz. the intellectual-lawyers, who possess the requisite social sensitivity, is powerless to wield any influence on the practising lawyers who must continue to pursue their profit interests.

It is better to live in a state of *clear* despair than to have an unreal hope. There is no point in celebrating the *promise of law* when all evidences are to the contrary. It will only be raising the structure of self-deception to the status of a demi-god. The political power functioning must leave law making and law reforms free and autonomous, capable of absorbing the orthogenetic compulsions of society and its needs. Also, the professional bodies must re-examine and re-state the professional lawyer's role in the light of new social goals and accordingly prepare their members – both for the bar and the bench. Only when these conditions are met, would law be the unchained Prometheus which it inherently is. But as yet, such a vista is a far cry, indeed a very far cry !

CHAPTER SEVEN

CULTURE OF CRIMINAL JUSTICE : A MICRO-LEVEL EXPLORATION

(A) INTRODUCTION : SETTING, METHODOLOGY AND PERSPECTIVE

THIS IS A brief and tentative write-up on the *culture* of criminal justice. It is a prelude to a fuller study which has been planned on the nature and type of criminal justice available at the criminal courts in India, especially the trial courts. The setting here is a district court location in the capital city of Delhi. So far, only an overall number of 50 respondents drawn from various categories of court-officials and law professionals have been interviewed between January-July, 1986. This number, however, does not include those whose mode of functioning and working was studied and observed informally rather than formally interviewing them. These include the law-tricksters or touts, lay-typists, stamp-vendors, scattered all along the court-corridors. Those interviewed formally, included the following:

(1) Lawyers.

(2) Public Prosecutors.

(3) Judges.

(4) Court officials such as readers, typists, *ahalmads*, peons and Naib-courts all formally a part of the trial-court bureaucracy.

(5) Police officials, especially those who bring the accused along to the trial court from the Police custody, on the day of the hearing.

As mentioned above, the purpose in this study is to explore some prominent contours of the CULTURE of criminal justice. In particular the emphasis is on such norms, values, stereotypes and perceptions, as are shared by a majority of the respondents drawn from the above categories. The CULTURE, which theoretically could have several referents, refers here in particular to the *generalized orientation*, which these personnel have towards the conduct of criminal Justice in these courts. Further, all these orientations explored here are not merely *cognitive* or *emotive* in nature, but instead find expression in their day-to day behaviour and attitude towards the accused, criminal litigation and also towards each other. Alternatively speaking, these orientations could be regarded as part and parcel of their culture.

The overall theoretical assumption guiding the study has been two-fold : first, that the nature of culture pervading the criminal litigation matters crucially in determining the quality of CRIMINAL JUSTICE and second, that this culture is structured and shaped in its primary-setting of trial courts, i.e. the very first level where criminal proceedings on a case are initiated. Looking to the exploratory character of this study and also to the limited scope of its investigations, we refrained from imposing any prior theoretical design or schema. Rather, it was allowed to emerge automatically from the nature and scope of observations. In specific, we found it almost inescapable to pursue a combination of *dramaturgical* (Goffman, 1974) and *participation observation* perspectives.

(B) THE DATA

This section has been divided into two parts. In part I, we shall present some representative dramaturgical situations involving various *actors* participating in the process of criminal justice that were observed at the trial-courts under question. In part II of the chapter, we shall record a few proto-typical interviews that were held with some of these actors—both individually and in group-sessions. Later, we shall try to bring these two together and draw some theoretical and substantive inferences. Both the dramaturgical situations and the interviews are selected for their representative and illustrative value, rather than as adequate samples.

I. Dramaturgical Situations

Dramaturgical Situation Number 1

A trial court of a Metropolitan Magistrate who is not present in the court; however, on both flanks of his seat are sitting, his reader and typist, conversing with relatives, friends or other connections of the accused who are about to appear in the court today. The two persons talking to the two court-functionaries do not belong to the same case, which is apparent from their manner of their mutual unconcern. I am standing close to the wooden partition which separates the judge-reader and typist, from the rest of the court-room quadrangle where the trial takes place. An elderly man of about 65, tall and well-dressed (a hotelier, as discovered later) is agitated with the reader, from the way he talks to him, alternating a filthy abuse with a leering smile, which signifies that both acknowledge very well their pre-existing intimacy.

> "Why, the case has not yet come up at all? After all, there is nothing in it. Just two hearings and it is all over. Police has nothing and can prove nothing against me. You are hardly a friend, rather, you are my enemy. You asked for a bottle and you got it....Be human and do something."
>
> "What is a bottle ? Is it worth only that much. You are too stingey and ungrateful. How long you think I can continue to serrve you having nothing ?"
>
> "O, come on, you son of a bitch; your stomach is like a well without any bottom. I will have you done with if you misbehave (laughingly). Just do as I want and as about your bottles and gifts, there will be no problem". (After this, the man pats the reader's shoulder slightly, both smile at each other, shake hands and the man leaves the court-room in the company of an un-impressive looking, youngish lawyer who had not uttered a single word while the two conversed with each other).

Dramaturgical Situation Number 2

The magistrate has not yet come. After a brief one hour session in the court he reportedly left for hospital in connection with the medication of his child. His reader knows me; so I sneak close to the wooden panel behind which he normally sits by the side of the magistrate. He is already in conversation with a lady—scantily dressed in her late forties or early fifties. She is talking through a 25 years old *munshi* (clerk) of her lawyer. She wants the hearing postponed, her counsel is out of Delhi. "Is it true", the reader asks. But, then, without waiting for her answer, quips "How can that be possible ? The whole court-justice would come crashing down if we keep on giving dates after dates". The youngman in the company of the lady looks meaningfully at the reader, who winks back without the lady knowing it.

The reader (to the lady) : I hope you understand, it is not that simple but I believe you that your counsel is out. (The man accompanying makes a gesture to the reader, who starts again)

> ..."Alright alright, write an application and send it through him (*i.e.* the clerk)...he will tell you whatever happens. Don't come yourself. Stay there on your lawyer's seat only."

II. Interviews

(b) *Interview No. 1*

(With Metropolitan Magistrate's Reader)

One Mr. Sharma is a reader to the court, which the present magistrate has joined about 2 years ago. Mr. Sharma is 52 years old and boasts of "having been in the system for the last 30 years". I have visited him twice in the court, when it is not in session and talked to him from across the wooden-panel, which separates the courtroom from the judge's seat—which is on an elevated plane. Mr. Sharma's seat is on the right-hand side of the judge's seat, whereas the typist flanks him on the left side. During the very first visit, Sharma starts out by saying that he is sick of the job now; he wants to do something else...some petty business. He admits that he makes about Rs. 15, Rs. 20 per working day but at the same time admits his relative limitation in accepting the 'consideration-money' since he cannot leave his seat and run after the 'parties' as easily as the typist, peon or the *ahalmad* do, implying the relative respectability of his position. The only way, he admits, that he is able to help the parties and make his side-earnings is by adjusting, re-adjusting the dates fixed for the cases or for getting adjournments.

> "...Of course, nothing can be done once the cause-list is prepared a day-before, but, a little before that, yes something is possible...I help the lawyers too, by getting the hearings postponed either because they are busy elsewhere or because the witnesses are not ready, or something like that. I can easily fix all this."
>
> I ask, "I am told that readers also help the accused by pulling out some 'crucial' papers from the case-files..."

The reader : (abruptly, and showing a little annoyance)

> "...Whoever told you all this ? You do not understand the basics of the criminal cases...you know, these papers are passed on to us by the police-*thana*, and are indexed on the front-page. One paper misplaced and you can even land up behind bars. No, no, this is simply not possible...no body does this...at any cost, whatsoever."

Even though Mr. Sharma seems happy with extra money he makes in addition to his salary, he does have some problem convincing his wife that the money so obtained is alright and could be used as a part of the domestic expenditure. His wife being a religious lady does not accept this contention. For example, Mr. Sharma reports of an incident when with the graft money of Rs. 500 that he had obtained from one of his clients, he wanted to purchase a ceiling-fan for the house. As he reports, his wife refused point-blank, fearing that the fan may even fall upon the family while they are asleep and hurt someone, since the money involved in the purchase was not of honest-earning. I ask Mr. Sharma, how he expends the extra-money, he reports that somehow it finds its way into the family, directly or indirectly. For example, clothes are purchased, white-washing and polishing of the house is done with the same money. And, whatever is left, he spends on his own entertainment and that of his friends.

Interview No. 2

I visit an Assistant Public Prosecutor (APP) in the room of his senior who allocates him work and also monitors its discharge. The overall setting is that of the Directorate of Public Prosecutor, occupying the right wing of the first floor of the court-building. Approximately, there are 20 rooms occupied by either the APPS or Senior PPS, or alternatively the Directorate's bureaucratic establishment. When I enter the room of my respondent, he is absent; instead, his senior is sitting alongwith his office-superintendent and taking stock of the progress of various cases which are to be pursued in the trial court by various (three) APPS working under his charge. The senior shows an extreme cordiality since I have come to ask some questions about the way, he and his department is working. While the conversation is on, we are joined by the concerned APP whom I have come to interview. He tells me apologetically that since there are no cases listed for the day, he is late in arriving. Just as he starts talking, an ASI (Assistant Sub-Inspector) comes in with two case-files on which to seek the opinion of the concerned APP i.e. whether to pursue the cases against persons charged or drop them. The APP starts examining the case-papers, which are just two bunches of loosely tagged papers, with index-sheets on top of each. There are no *folders* or *files* in which these papers are placed. While the APP is turning the papers, some of the documents are loosening and coming off the bunches.

> "Why are these documents not properly put into the folders", I ask.
>
> "...You should rather ask, whether there are proper chairs and tables, fans and water-pitchers in the *thana*" The APP tells me. "Have you ever gone to a thana...I mean. In any

connection? ...These people have a miserable life. It is impossible in many police-stations to spend an hour, where these people have to spend 12 hours...Take the case of this ASI" (alluding to ASI, who has come with the files) "The S.H.O. will not have a look at him and will abuse him hard and sound unless he brings these files back to *thana* with our notings. That's why I am doing it even though these cases are not marked to me". "But, why should his S.H.O., be so particular about these cases", I ask him.

"Personal interest...he may be in league with the aggrieved party and thus, want to help him against the accused...or he may even be wanting to help the accused and quickly get him out, knowing that the FIR would not clearly hold him guilty and he would, therefore, get the benefit of doubt...."

He is purusing the papers, while talking to me, and keeps reprimanding the ASI lightly for the incomplete documents and statements made by witnesses. Finally, he pens down his opinions on both the cases and puts these before his senior who initials them and hands the files over to the waiting ASI. Just when the latter is leaving the room, the senior P.P. asks:

"...Is Kishan Lal* at Karim Ganj thana* these days"
"Yes, Sab, he is very much there...Anything ?" the ASI asks.

"Yes a little help".

"No problem Sir, he is dependable". The senior P.P. looks at him and then averts his gaze on becoming conscious that I was attentive to their conversation.

An hour later, the same situation

A head-constable is standing by the table of the Sr. PP. while he is looking through a file brought with the help of his assistant. I am engaged in conversation with my own respondent, but I notice that he (i.e. the senior PP) is reprimanding the head-constable on some issue again and again. The office peon comes into the room and

*fictitious names.

passes some message to the APP, I am talking to. He goes out of the room to talk to two persons standing outside the room in the corridor, visible from the seat where I am sitting. Meanwhile, the head-constable with whom the Sr. P.P. was getting annoyed, goes out of the room, the Sr. P.P. addresses me :

> "...It will perhaps surprise you to know that this case will be time-barred in another one week...and this has reached me only today...By the time, we advise the *thana*, it will be all over...a dead case".
>
> "But why should it happen like this," I ask.
>
> "The guess is so very simple...The police after filing the FIR against the accused, developed some understanding with him, and now wants to help him....But they must have taken a fat sum, since they will have to explain delay on their own part also...."

He bemoans that he is over-worked and over a hundred cases are pending under his charge, and also that neither the office-bureaucracy nor the police-station from where the cases come are of much help. His office-staff keeps the files with them for weeks on-end after these are received from the police *Thana*. Even when the files finally arrive on his seat, he finds them incomplete. Even the copies of the statements of various witnesses recorded by the police are not complete, clear and legible. Sometimes he finds very serious lacunae in the way, cases have been processed by the Police Officers. He also mentions about the indifferent attitude of some of the APPS working under his charge. He is not able to pursue this point further since the APP who had gone out has now returned.

While re-starting his conversation, the APP is slightly uneasy and a bit nervous. Nevertheless, following is the near-exact sequence of our conversation. I take the initiative :

> "So many people need your advice...were they some personal friends who had come to see you".
>
> (He does not get annoyed at this interfering question; instead. replies)

"No, they came through a friend—Do you know what they were asking for ? They wanted me to certify a marriage, which they knew I won't be able to attend on account of my pre-occupations elsewhere—Now, I don't know whether or not this marriage is going to take place at all on that day—I refused and asked them to request the marriage-magistrate for this."

"What kind of professional relations you have with your colleagues who are practising in the district courts here" ?

"Surely, not as close as they have among themselves, but I do go and sit in the bar-room though I am not supposed to be a member of the district court bar association—Besides, there are also some other courtesies which are often exchanged between us—"

"Like what ?"

"Well, a case may come to me for my advice from a *thana*. If pursued, the case may not be able to stand a single hearing and may be instantly dismissed on being brought to trial. So, the proper advice to the SHO should be to drop the case. But the defence counsel who stands engaged on the case may persuade me to at least commit the case to trial so that he may get something out of it. Even if there is instant acquittal on the first hearing, the counsel would benefit since he would have one more 'victory' to his credit."

"But is it not un-professional since it goes against the interest of the accused. Do you think judges also extend such courtesies to those involved in criminal litigation."

"Yes, a majority of them do though not on all cases; a judge may guide the counsel of an accused to present the case in a certain manner which will weaken the prosecutor's case."

"Where does all this transaction take place ?"

"In the judge's chamber or even in his house—normally, the advice is passed on through a common connection."

Interview No. 3 (Interview with a magistrate)

Mr. Singh is 38 years old and is a metropolitian magistrate. He possesses BA (Honours) degree in English in addition to graduation in law. As he reported, he had joined judiciary for achieving an honourable status and also for proving to his family that he could become a judge. Sometime in the middle of October, '86, I met him in his ante-room during one afternoon when he had temporarily retired from the day's work. I confronted him with the popular prespective—including that of the public prosecutors, on the lower judiciary that most of them were accepting 'money' or some 'gifts' for the favours extended to lawyers and clients. He retorted :

> "...I cannot vouche for everybody who is a judge or a magistrate in this court, that he or she is incorruptible, but I can tell you that this is beyond my comprehension as to how could one be possibly a corrupt judge. I am aware of impressions circulating around...but then this is the average morality in our society, otherwise how would the courts be chocked with arrears ? Let's not forget that in view of the mounting load of cases that one has to attend to, judgements are not an everyday affair. So, justice is delayed. Also, to each victory on a case, there is a corresponding defeat of some one. All this nurtures enough basis for suspicion, regret and malicious slander. The only lapse of which a judge, here, sometime may be accused of is that he may not be able to concentrate enough on a case...and that is only on account of unmanageable load of work, which he may have, and the resulting fatigue or strain. If the court-staff or the prosecutors accuse judges of impropriety, it is only because they themselves are corrupt...."

(C) INFERENCES AND SEMI-INFERENCES

As explained in the preceding, this has been a very limited exploration into cultural components of criminal justice at a district setting in the capital city of Delhi. Further, we also mentioned that *culture* in our context has a specific connotation, i.e. it refers to the general attitude and orientation which various participants in the criminal justice have towards criminal litigation, the system and process of justice involved therein, and also towards each other. The methodology used here is the one, suited to the nature and range of this limited inquiry. The various court-situations observed and unstructed interviews conducted led us heuristically to a combination of *Goffmanian dramaturgy* and the well-known anthropological technique of *participant observation.* Several situations were observed and recorded over the past six months. Those reported here are relatively more composite and representative of the kind of ethos—impinging upon the nature of criminal justice, which various participants share among themselves. Looking to the 'pilot' nature of this study, no tall claim is intended or can be made as to the all-India validity of some of the suggestions and semi-inferences being stated hereunder. Nevertheless, given the fact that the institutional framework of criminal justice in the country is a representation of the legal system which was evolved and followed over the past two hundred years, the cultural uniformities, if not identities are bound to be found between the various micro-settings in the country. As such, the relevance of their mention here. Some of the leading orientations constitutive of this culture as in our usage here, are as follows :

1. There is a common attitude of un-concern on the part of all the participants towards the accused, the procedure and process of criminal litigation and consequently the nature and quality of criminal justice. First of all, lawyers look upon the criminal litigant as a usable and expendable source, fit only for generation of pecuniary benefits. They are often indifferent in making court-appearance on the dates on which their cases have been fixed already. Seemingly, they prefer to attend to such cases as are listed in relatively higher courts, such as the Sessions Court, because the cases involved there are of more serious type such as those involving charges of murder and rape. This is putatively so, because they fetch them higher fees and other extortions from their clients. They collude apparently and clearly with the court-staff in getting postponments of the hearings at the lower courts i.e. Metropolitan Courts. The magistrates, we observed did not seem to exercise absolute control over the court-calender, thus

giving free-way to the court-staff for complicity both with the defence-counsels and the accused for the alteration and re-fixation of dates.

2. For the court-staff, accused is nothing but a milch-cattle to be bled white through a variety of extortions all along the progress of a case, for a variety of real or imaginary services rendered. These may include production of the case-file at the appropriate time, adjustment of the dates, reading out to the witness the statement made earlier by him to the police, now just before he takes the witness-stand in the court. The court officials were also found creating unreal fears in the minds of the accuseds and those accompanying them, as to the direction a case was likely to take in the court for the sake of extracting money. Even after aquittal the accused is not let off, but instead, fleeced for gift-payments to the court-staff. What is shocking is not merely the prevailance of such practices, but that they prosper under the very nose of the judges, indifference on whose part is suggestive either of complicity, incapacity or of professional neglect. Dramaturgy observed and analysed in the preceding, brings out in clear relief the laconic casualness with which the professionals pursue their business of administering and pursuing justice.

3. The study also brings out the attitude of bureaucratic neglect on the part of 'prosecution' limb of the criminal justice which seems to go on somehow like an over-fed machine, on the verge of crack and collapse. For APPs and, PPs, criminal cases constitute just an avoidable strain and burden, and hence they do barely enough to keep their jobs. Much of their energy, they seem to be employing for socialising for their personal benefits. There are also suggestions that some criminal cases are killed on account of collusion and complicity between the police and prosecution in the interest of the accused. Therefore, for meeting the ends of criminal justice—which is indeed the responsibility which legal system owes towards society, all these overt and covert complicities spell disaster. The quality of criminal justice is thus, pulled down to its palpably low level.

4. Virtually, all the professional role-categories (i.e. lawyers, lawyer-prosecutors and judges) as well as the bureaucratic parapher-

nalia of the court-system, engaged in dispensing criminal justice hold mutual antipathies and hostile stereotypes. But, all the same, through their attitude of neglect, apathy and self-gratification, they all seem to be working towards the same end : Neglect and denial of criminal justice. This consequence remains un-altered whether an accused is favoured against the state or vice-versa. The culture of casualness, complicity and concurrence represented and practised by the professionals in criminal litigation is out-of-step with the high quality of criminal justice that one may ideally expect. Probably, the deeper sociological analysis of this malaise must compell us pay attention to some of the more basic reasons, such as the backdrop of poverty and economic-insufficiency, the culture of administrative *ad-hocism* as a carry-over of the colonial legacy, and incomplete socialization of professionals and bureaucrats in the values and orientations, which are inseparable adjuncts of the ideal justice-system.

5. In terms of Goffmanian dramaturgy, the situations observed in the study bring out a contrasting "presentation of self" on the part of *professional* and *bureaucratic* role-categories. The former i.e. the lawyers, prosecutors and judges are found "apparently" conforming to their expected behaviour and are thus, able to save their "identity" from being damaged publicly and irretrievably. The bureaucratic role-categories on the other hand, openly flout norms of expected behaviour and almost totally erode even the minimal semblance of their "role identity". But despite this apparent *dramatic* constraint on the part of law-professionals for an adherence to the outward form of their expected role-behaviour, the invisible components of their professional role-discharge provide them a substantial *back-stage*[1] (Goffman, 1974) facility for obviating the substantive canons of commitment to litigants, the court-system and to the wider society. In terms of their dysfunctionality, both are *integral*, nay even *symbiotic* in constituting and perpetuating an anti-culture i.e. a culture "anti" to the needs of dispensing justice in society.

1. E. Goffman, *The Presentation of Self in Everyday Life*, London, Penguin Books, (1974).

6. On the policy-front, all the above inferences have a pointed bearing in suggesting that the reformers of Indian Legal scene have sorely neglected the micro-most legal setting i.e. the trial courts, at whose doors the huge chunk of the litigants' collectivity knock for quick and fair justice. Notwithstanding several recent moves on the part of a few members of the higher judiciary and the top bar, to activate the legal system in order to provide justice to the poor and the deprived in keeping with the spirit of basic principles of the state policy, the un-wary and the un-informed continue to be a mere *powder* under the grinding stone of inequity and injustice. What is the elites' thinking on these 'micro' yet highly 'central' matters?

CHAPTER EIGHT

PHENOMENOLOGY OF EMERGENT CULTURE: THE CASE OF INDIAN LAWYERS AND LEGAL SYSTEM

INTRODUCTION AND BACKGROUND

THIS IS PURPORTED to be a tentative outline of a fuller study of the emergent culture of the Indian legal profession. The said culture is emerging not only among the practising lawyers, but also among the judiciary, law-writers and columnists and also among the teaching segment of the legal profession. The term "profession" thus is used here a little indefensibly, since it refers not merely to those who "practise in the service of clients in a court of law" or give them consultations on legal matters, but also to those who adjudicate law, i.e. the judiciary. The barest common denominator among all these, however, is that they are trained *lawyers* or hold degrees in law, no matter what use they make of this training in their occupation or in making their livelihood. In the context of the legal or professional culture that is shaping up, there is, however, an unmistakable similarity in their perspectives and orientations in that they all choose to put a particular meaning and purpose on law and its relevance in society, in explicit and manifest terms. This is precisely the justification for arguing that their ideas and orientations point toward a similar direction or that they effort to forge and nurture the same complex of ideas and values. That is why all these categories of professionals can be thought of as collaborators in the same and similar effort. All this, however, does not imply that the said culture has come to stay or will stabilise in the near or distant future. The process triggered by the said cultural configuration may meet its match eventually either through strategic re-organization of the opposing interests that now come under threat or through internal divisions or fissions among the various participants of the emerging cultural drama. Alternatively, the threatened social interests may achieve a myriad variety of mutual accommodations with the obtrusive parameters of this emergent culture.

The culture under mention may be called the culture of *positive criticality*; and, in this brief paper, we propose to discuss the *phenomenology* of this culture, i.e. try to identify such phenomena and processes, through which this culture is composed, constituted and then sought to be stabilized. However, before we enter upon the main thesis, the term "positive criticality" needs to be explicated. "Criticality", here, has a referent in the entire *Legal System*. It may refer to the law—its form, procedure, attitude or orientation and adjudication, the legal procedure, attitude or orientation of the judiciary towards the litigation or the litigants, or towards the overall frame of legitimacy or the constitution within which all issues are sought to be settled. The criticality here may refer to either of these or all, and to some other related constituents also. The criticality inheres the attitudes of various segments of legal profession, who point out the contemporaneous unsuitability of the legal system both in its structure-composition as well as day-to-day operation. But the criticism of the legal system that is built up by above-listed categories is not an exercise in itself, but instead intended to prepare basis for some creative agenda, which if carried, would rectify the systemic unsuitability or its anachronistic character. Also, these prescriptive suggestions are followed up by professionals themselves through carrying out some fundamental transformations in their own professional conduct and role-discharge. For all such reasons, therefore, the criticality is positive, and not *negative* or merely condemnatory.

The genesis of this growing culture stretches back to not earlier than the last ten years or so. Even though, one needs to dig into last hundred and fifty years in order to affirm the recency of these origins, yet it is not difficult to see that the crucial determinant of this phenomenon is only the post independence (or post, 1947) dialectics and contradictions between the pre-existing legal system and legal culture on the one hand and the contemporary problematics, on the other. The fact that even after the independence of the country, this dialectics or awareness of incongruity took thirty years to formalize itself, is a matter requiring a more systematic analysis into a variety of socio-political events and their impact upon the professionals. All this analysis is being undertaken by the author separately ; yet, for the time, an unequivocal argument can be made that there is such a process afoot as the emergence of a new culture and that it is likely to have a strong impact upon the state of things to come in society. Sky-rocketing social aspirations may be raised—which may be fulfilled or thwarted. In the process, a new profile of relationship may emerge between the profession and the polity. But, alternatively, unable to realize its objectives, this new cultural ebullience may die down out of sheer dissipation of effort and the resultant ennui and frustration of the participant categories. But, all this is for the future to unfold ; we can only sketch the probabilities that lie ahead.

We shall now proceed to present the substantive data on the aforesaid two dimensions of this emerging culture of criticality, viz. the critique of the legal system, and the suggested improvisations and innovations both in the legal system and in the professional orientations of the lawyers and judges.

CRITIQUE OF THE LEGAL SYSTEM—ITS LEGITIMATION ETC.

I would like to state at the very outset that the members of the profession—as identified above, i.e. academics, lawyers, judges and the law-columnists, selected here are merely illustrative of the category to which they belong. It neither means that there are none others than these, nor that these represent a fair sample of the professional category to which they belong. It only means that they are perhaps ideal-typical of their specific sub-categories vis-a-vis the culture under mention. There may also be a certain bias of selectivity; but this may have un-willingly resulted from my incomplete awareness about the full range of professionals in each category.

We start with the critical perspectives on the legal system, by the law-academics; and illustratively we report from the observations of a well-known law-academic—Upendra Baxi on the crisis afflicting the Indian legal system (Baxi 1982).

(*i*) He bemoans the fact that there is a near-complete collapse of the legitimacy of the contemporary legal system in India. The system is disregarded with compunction by the political elite who rather use it as an instrument in their power game. The same behavioural pattern percolates down to the people who regard law more as an "irritating inconvenience" to be avoided and bypassed, if possible, rather than as a facility for an orderly conduct of social life. Endemic corruption—both economic and political, abuse and often over-use of power, buttresses this tendency all the more. Organized countervailing power as manifested through both violent and non-violent variety of agitation-politics, notwithstanding their utility in uncovering governmental lapses, further erodes the legitimacy of the legal system. Various agitating groups use the high danger-quotient of their direct action strategy to pressurise the administration into submission. As a result, politics by manipulation comes to be regarded as the dependable strategy. All this entails erosion of legitimacy of the legal system. As pointed out by Baxi, it is not just the agitating groups from the general public who resort to manipulation, and disregard of the law. Rather, the government also disregards the law both through non-implementation and also through distortion and mis-representation. What is piognant is the governments' own weak or low-level commitment to legalism or the rule of law. The Chasnala mine disaster involving substitute labour, a practice forbidden by law, occurred in the nationalized sector. The Contract Labour (Abolition) Act does not apply to the public sector. The government goes right up to the Supreme Court protesting against compensation awarded to the widow of people killed in accidents while performing governmental duty and the defence of sovereign immunity. Recently, the state of Haryana appealed to the Court against the decision of the High Court liberating the widow of a person, run over by a Haryana bus from paying court fees (she could not afford this). A law passed by the Kerala legislature to provide certain benefits to casual and temporary workers two years ago is still awaiting union governments' clearance. It is not forthcoming because of the apprehension that if this law is extended to central employees, a huge financial liability will arise, which may be particularly aggravated if this 'contagion' spreads to other states.

(*ii*) Baxi follows up this critique of legitimacy by a critique of the various components of the legal system itself. Here, he points out certain antinomies and contradictions within the Indian Constitution, the legal system etc. This is both by mutually inconsistent legal provisions as well as through an antipathy between the provisions as inscribed within the Constitution and the way they are actualized. For example, despite the constitutional objectives of equality, fraternity, liberty, dignity, justice, the law-making, law-enforcement and adjudication continue to have a backward orientation. Also, despite strong constitutional emphasis on developing decentralization of political power through the principle of federalism, the Centre continues to wield almost unlimited power vis-a-vis the states. Also, the actual operation of the Constitution over the years, for example, has not resulted in any set of restraining conventions on the constitutional power of the Union of India to declare *Presidents' Rule* in the states and to impose *emergencies*. Further, no conventions regarding such matters as the appointment of Chief Justice of India and appointment and transfer of judges, declaration of emergencies and election expenses, etc.. have so far been evolved. All these tend to create continuing uncertainties and dilemmas in the ILS (Indian Legal System) and in the political system.

He also elucidates the principle of *legal liberalism* which ought to be followed by all liberal polities as enunciated by Max Weber, to be constitutive of *Positivistic* nature of law and its foundation on *social consensus*, the essentially *impersonal* nature of compliance and obedience, etc. All these components, he says, are in utter neglect in the Indian context. Baxi, also highlights the stranglehold of the colonial legal system over the Indian Legal System, in

1. Upendra Baxi : Crisis in Indian Legal System, Vikas Pub., New Delhi, 1882.

that both law-making, law-implementation continue to follow the non-participative, 'top-down' model being the exclusive preserve of a microscopic elite. The people at large in various organizational forums such as *panchayats* or various other prominent social institutions such as Universities, Bar, media, other organized groups and voluntary bodies, etc., fail to play any useful part, since they are not consulted by law-making agencies.

> There are occasional sermons that people should help the state make the laws effective, that they should not withhold active co-operation from the law-enforcement agencies, that they should develop a civic competence, a stake in the maintenance of social control and promotion of social change. All this rhetoric is no doubt nobly inspired but the legal systems as structured provide little or no effective scope for public participation in the implementation of legislation... Broadly, the ILS follows the colonial model of reactive mobilization of the law rather than pro-active mobilization.[1(i)]

The same colonial model is followed with regard to citizens' access to law. Sometimes, even the barest information on a law is difficult to come by.

> Normative law is virtually inaccessible to the most under-privileged and vulnerable groups in Indian society—legal illiteracy of the beneficiaries of law, thus contributes to its ineffectiveness, e.g. : prisoners may not even get to see the jail manuals when distinguished criminologists find it extremely hard to get a copy. Neither the bonded labour nor the landless labour have much idea of the law and the uses that can be made of it.[1(ii)]

Even, the Judiciary, pays obeisance to this policy of withholding information. There is no developed system followed by the Supreme Court of sharing information on decisions and judgements given, with its subordinate High Courts. Not merely that, the

1(i) *Ibid.*, p. 47.
1(ii) *Ibid.*, pp. 49-50.

Supreme Court follows the dubious practice of "classifying" certain decisions, so that information on them need not be made open.

> "...A leading law publisher who has unsuccessfully tried to get the judgements of the Supreme Court 'Classified,' found that during the 1950-55 period, as many as 250 decisions were classified by the Court as 'non-reportable'."[1(iii)]

Another telling evidence of the perpetuating colonial character of Indian Legal Sytem lies in that even the right of indigent clients to courts, was recognized quite belatedly, and when it was done, both the state and the profession showed very little enthusiasm in participating in the formulation of comprehensive scheme. Ludicrously enough, as Baxi maintains, the reason accounted for by the government is the insufficiency of finance. That, the legal aid to the indigent client should automatically follow from his fundamental right of equality before the law, did not occur to the state through all these years.

After all these critical comments on the declining legitimacy and the un-responsive character of the Indian Legal System, he now sets out to examine its chief institutional components such as courts; police; law-reform commission; jail administration. He concludes through a comprehensive persual of all these that they are characterized respectively by slowness; retrogression; *ad-hocism* and casualness and, a violent disregard for the Manual-Rules of propriety and humanism. A general strand running through his entire critique of the Indian Legal System brings home the dual message; first, that the system is not likely to collapse under the weight of its own degeneration as is generally thought it would, on account of its pliability in the hands of the better-off and the *status quoist*, and second, that one way it can acquire a certain meaningfulness is through its integration with some of the time-honoured traditional Indian institutions, such as the *panchayats or nyaya panchayats*, which need to be activated in view of the collapse of legitimacy of the formal west-based legal institutions.

1(iii) *Ibid*, p. 50.

Towards alternatives

As a counter to retrogressive use of the law and law courts by the better-off sections of society against the defenceless, poor and uninformed-especially those living in the rural areas, he recommends the vigorous and instrumental use of the law by the legal activists to bring justice to these neglected sections of society.

Thus :

> Unless legal activists emerge, the gulf between courts and poor must remain almost the same. And the emergence of legal activists, whether academics, lawyers or judges, is itself problematic and contingent. India has witnessed its first real upsurge of legal activists (including even among justices of the Supreme Court) only in the past four years. This can be explained by the catharsis of middle and upper middle classes and their slight radicalisation, in the wake of and upon the cessation of the internal emergency in 1977 and the tumultuous populism of the Janata years and the return of Indira Gandhi.[2]

He also has another revolutionary proposal on hand to rectify the oddities in the functioning of the present legal system, i.e. popular participation in law-making. He says :

> Popular participation in law-making will not merely be of a reactive kind. It would enhance the possibility that groups of people might formulate legislative proposals for public discussion and legislative consideration. The latter is almost impossible in many Third World Societies. Procedures of law-making (petitions and private members' bills) almost preclude popular ventures in initiation of legislative proposals. In any event, it is plausible that peoples' participation in law-making (whether reactively or provocatively) will enhance their legal and political self-reliance. They will also enhance civic competence and social responsibility.[3]

2. Upendra Baxi, "Legal Mobilization and the Needs of the Rural Poor", in *Public Interest Litigation* : Some *Introductory Readings*, Ministry of Law, New Delhi, 1982 (mimeo), p. 12 (Part III).
3. *Ibid.*

Besides Upendra Baxi, there are a few more academics like Dr. Dhagamwar and others who provide a critique of the system and suggestions of reform along similar lines. Some like Baxi himself have also been engaged in some class-litigation cases as legal activists and have won notable successes in bringing relief to the affected people. Dr. Vasudha Dhagamwar, an ex-law teacher of Poona University and currently a social activist, has successfully defended the land rights of the tribals of Akkalkua a tehsil of Dhullia district of Maharashtra state and saved these people from an impossible prospect of having to pay for the purchase of same pieces of land for the second time. Eventually, she was responsible for having this issue settled once for all by having it included in the 9th Schedule of the Indian Constitution, on which no more litigation was possible. The tribal farmers were now free from all further payments. She started operating almost without any organized group of social activists and was able to achieve the desired mobilization of the people around this issue by promoting adequate involvement of the press and some public spirited people.[3(i)] The whole account reads indeed as a very brave effort of an academic.

So infectious has been the effect of this pro-poor instrumentation of the legal institutions on the part of academics, lawyers, judges and others, that even some notable scholars whose critique of legal system earlier was confined to the legal procedure or to the manner and method of interpretation of the law by the Supreme Court, or its ineptness in handling the issue of arrears, were eventually sucked into this slowly but steadily growing movement of Public Interest Litigation., For example, Mr. Rajiv Dhavan, in his earlier works has been confined to such like issues only as cited above, and has defended a conservative attitude to law-making, on the part of Supreme Court. For example, while discussing the role of "The Court as reformer",[3(ii)] he maintains :

3(i) Vasudha Dhagamwar, "Public Interest Litigation in Tenancy Matters", in *Ibid.*

3(ii) Rajiv Dhavan, The Supreme Court of India, 1977.

"One cannot help thinking that the reform must proceed from the people and not from notions of reform entertained by the Judges" (p. 45).

Eventually, he came to develop a strong interest in public interest litigation movement and has even served as a consultant to the Ministry of Law in suggesting an institutional format to achieve this end.

He maintains in the said report that legal help to the disadvantaged must extend beyond pre-occupation with litigation, which is forced upon them. They must be helped to actually achieve *entitlements* which are available to them within the law. He also terms these as "opportunity entitlements".

"...But there is a vast area of opportunity entitlements which are forgotten as the repression of the disadvantage meanders through the contours of the much manipulated local state. These are usually treated as a system of discriminatory largesses. These include a large number of areas like land distribution, the right to wages, minimum wages, fair conditions at work, the right not to be discriminated against, the right to positive discrimination in favour of certain cases and classes of cases, the right to food, the right to rations, the right to water, the right to credit, the right to agricultural developments to facilitate agricultural growth and investment, the right to education. Many of these have already been built into governmental legislation. Administrative machinery has been designed to ensure the delivery of those entitlements. A combination of administrative entropy and local manipulation direct and redistribute these entitlements so that they do not reach those for whom they are meant."[3(ii)]

Matching these two positions taken by Rajiv Dhavan in 1976 and 1982 respectively, one may ask : firstly why does he propose such a revolutionary role for the *lawyer*, and a basically conservative role for a *judge*, and secondly, can a radical or poor-oriented lawyer achieve anything against *locus standi* judges, who only

3(ii) Rajiv Dhavan, "From Litigation to Entitlements" in *Public Interest Litigation : Some Introductory Readings, op. cit.*, p. 18 (Part III).

interpret law without in the least bothering to *make* it. Obviously, it is only a case of successive coloration of the conventional values of a lawyer in the dye of growing radicalisation, which is seemingly spilling around. Once again, Dhavan's is only an illustrative case. There are several others.

PRACTISING LAWYERS

Besides the academics, there are also some practising lawyers who are strongly committed to this non-conventional type of litigation, called the Public Interest Litigation. They work within the framework of some Institutional nexus or the other, ranging from a husband-wife dyad (*e.g.* Nirmal Hingorani and Kapila Hingorani practising in Supreme Court of India) to one or more lawyers working collaboratively and attached to an ideologically committed platform which may be constituted of either the lawyers themselves such as the LAWYERS' COLLECTIVE of Bombay (which is expressly committed to the ideology of communism) or a Civil Liberties forum such as People's Union for Civil Liberties (PUCL) or People's Union for Democratic Rights (PUDR). The latter type of institutions include not merely the lawyers but also some other public spirited men and even members of the teaching profession and journalists. The institutional dynamics of these or other organizational forms is as yet under closer study and analysis, but the orientation and concern of lawyers working with them is clear enough and has a three-fold dimension. First, all these are highly critical and perceptive of the way the entire legal system including the judiciary works to the disfavour of the disadvantaged; and second, they are also conscious of the egalitarian potential of the constitution and the various laws that have been formulated in pursuance of these objectives. Thirdly, they litigate on behalf of the poor for various inequities suffered by them in violation of their fundamental rights guaranteed under the constitution. And, thus seeking through the courts the remedy against a specific wrong suffered by them, they are, as if, seeking the restoration of the fundamental right or rights. For example, in the now famous case of Bombay Pavement Dwellers, who were sought to be evicted by the municipal authorities from the pavements which they had occupied for quite some time and started using as a nexal point for earning their livelihood, both PUCL and the Lawyers' Collective of Bombay, defended their right to stay on the pavement as a remedy against a possible infringement of their fundamental right to earn their livelihood through a threatened eviction by the authorities. Hence, they argued that they cannot be displaced from here without providing them a composite alternative, which provides this dual facility of dwelling and earning. Of course, the recent judgement of the Supreme Court did not regard this as a tenable argument and ordered these dwellers to vacate the pavements, since otherwise the rights of the trespassers would be compromised. But, even at this, the Lawyers' Collective is not disheartened. Their president, Ms. Indira Jaising in a recent interview with me averred :

> "...I know that the Supreme Court has erred, and we are filing another petition."

It is very interesting to see that the position taken by two groups on the same case—notwithstanding the fact that both may be imbued with the zeal to do some good to the affected people, show subtle shades of ideological variations. Note, for example, what Ms. Indira Jaising had to say about the position taken on the case of dwellers by another action group PUCL—through their representative lawyer, Mr. Ashok Desai.

> "...He did a great damage to the case of the pavement dwellers by conceding in the court that even though these people should be provided alternative dwellings, they in fact had no right under the Constitution to occupy the pavements... whereas our position has been totally opposed to it, *i.e.* their eviction would mean infringement of their fundamental rights...."

Another member of the Collective put this positional difference between the two groups in clearer ideological perspective :

> "In clear terms we argue such cases from the standpoint of the proletarian class, whereas groups like PUCL maintain a middle class posture...For example, we have been maintaining on this case that they must be provided alternative dwellings before they are evicted, whereas the PUCL makes no such insistence."

There probably are several more differences between groups like the Collective on the one hand and those like PUCL or PUDR on the other, besides their manifest ideological difference, as stated above. All these, as I said, above are under minuter observation and analysis, and further results may be available only subsequently.

The lawyers working with the forums like PUCL and PUDR have a relatively free-floating position with regard to their professional practice. They choose to work on cases they feel seized with, and unlike the members of the Collective having a "joint" or a "shared" practice in the larger sense of the term, pursue their individual practice in the way they feel like. They also do not make a fetish of excluding certain categories of legal business. For example, the members of the "Collective" in a recent interview with me maintained that they never take the case of an employer against his employee, or that of a husband against an aggrieved wife. Against this, Mr. V.M. Tarkunde, president of the PUCL and Mr. Gobinda Mukhoty of the PUDR (both of whom are working as 'senior' counsels at Supreme Court) were quite candid in admitting that they did not declare certain cases out of bounds for themselves, even though through the kind of professional reputation they enjoyed, an employer would be discouraged from engaging them. As Mr. Mukhoty said :

> "...Having known my strong socialist and Marxist views, and the kind of arguments I make in defending the aggrieved employees in a court of law, any employer would think several times before coming to me...even then, I must say that I do not make a fetish of excluding certain cases."

So, was Mr. V.M. Tarkunde's argument while defending the case of the Children Society of Bombay versus a known social activist of Bombay, Ms. Sheela Barse :

> "...She is making all kinds of accusations against the Society that it is misusing the funds granted to it by the state and depriving children...I don't feel apologetic that I am representing this Society against a section of children who are

alleged to be ill-treated. Among many points to be considered in this case is, whether the childrens' interests will not be adversely effected if the Society were to be denied all financial help..."

The relatively more intellectual among the practising lawyers who have taken to Public Interest Litigation realize the necessity of this litigation on account of two fundamental reasons. Firstly, there is a lag or continuing chasm between the promise of equalitarianism and egalitarianism as enshrined in the Constitution (*e.g.* through Directive Principles of the State Policy exhorting the State to move towards granting to the individuals, 'right to work', 'education for all', 'public assistance to the indigent persons', 'equal pay for equal work' on the one hand, and the reality of day-to-day situation in the country, on the other. Gobinda Mukhoty,[3(iii)] instances some of the glaring violations of the fundamental rights as follows ;

— *Report in the Guardian, U.K., 1979* : India having per capita income of Rs. 120 per month was almost at the bottom of the list (in comparison Kuwait has Rs. 12,500 per capita income per month).

— *A news item on April 28, 1981* : Kamla, part of humanity's flotsam, rejected by her brothers and in-laws was sold at last for Rs. 2300 in flesh market of Madhya Pradesh, situated opposite the circuit house.

— *November 3, 1982* : India has 7 million bonded labourers, a Report of the anti-slavery society submitted to U.N. Working Group.

— According to the recent Planning Commission Report, nearly 240 million people live below poverty line.

Secondly, the intellectual lawyers are acutely conscious of this, that despite the fact that the Indian State has formally conceded certain fundamental "human rights" to its wider citizenry in pur-

---

3(iii) Gobinda Mukhoty, "Human Rights and Civil Liberties" A note collected personally and prepared for publication in a Law Journal.

suance of United Nations Charter of Human Rights of 1984, they have quite often been breached. Illustrating several instances taken both from Congress I—led as well as Janta Party—led governments at the centre, he cites several instances of the flagrant violations of rights. Some of these as listed by him as follows :

17-3-1980	"A procession of blind people waiting to go to the Prime Minister's house was brutally lathicharged by the police."
15-6-1980	"Police killings that shook a village."
26-6-1980	"Woman paraded naked, then raped by police."
24-8-1980	"3000 times a police witness."
22-11-1980	"Bihar 'Final' solution for Crime : Blind Under-trial."
27-11-1980	"Eyes punctured twice to ensure total blindness."
27-9-1981	"Lucknow : the tribals mainly live on leaves for three to four months a year."
17-12-1981	"Convicts turned into mental cases due to torture."
7-3-1983	"Nothing to eat but poisonous weeds."

THE JUDICIARY

The articulation and actualization of the lawyers' concern for the 'spirit' of the Constitution and for the Civil rights and liberties of the citizens, cannot make much headway against a judiciary that is doggedly *status quoist* and staunchly adheres to the formal letter of the law. It is only during the last 5-6 years that some of the judges —part of higher judiciary, i.e. working in the Supreme Court of India, have shown explicit concern for considering and even conceding the claims of the poor and the disadvantaged to file a case without a full compliance to the rules and procedures of the court. Some of the main orientations of such judges are as follows :

(i) Critique of the System

First of all they are bitterly critical of the Indian Legal System, as inherited from the colonial masters, because as the system exists currently, it is unable to meet the needs of the Indian people, most of whom are poor, apathetic to their own lot and un-informed.

> "...If law must serve life—the life of the many, million masses whose lot has been blood, toil, tears and sweat—the crucifixion of the Indo-Anglican system and the resurrection of the Indian system is an imperative of Independence."[4]

or more specifically

> "...Anglo-Sexon law is transactional, highly individualistic concerned with an atomistic justice incapable of responding to the claims and demands of collectivity, and resistant to change. Such law was developed and has developed in an essentially individualistic society to deal with situations involving the private right/duty pattern. It cannot possibly meet the challenge raised by the new concerns for the social rights and collective claims of the under-privileged. What we, therefore, need to do is to fashion new strategies – in fact, evolve a new jurisprudence—and find a new policy of collectivity as a backdrop to our efforts."[5]

Sometimes, the rhetoric from judiciary on the theme of reaching and relating law to the people is reminiscent of a Jacobites, fighting in the name of 'reason' in a political club during the revolutionary France of eighteenth century.

> "...We cannot allow the power of law to be cornered by the tycoons, the litigationists and the corporations which, as Lord Coke noticed centuries ago 'cannot commit treason, nor be outlawed, nor ex-communicated, *for they have no souls*'. These soulless giants oppress the worker and the consumer, pollute air and water all environment, and corrupt those in political power in all the branches so that a high tide of

4. V.R., Krishna Iyer, *Indian Justice*, Vedpal Law House, Indore, 1984, pp. 6-7.
5. P.N. Bhagwati, "Judicial Activism and Public Interest Litigation", *Address* delivered at the Columbia University School of Law, and published in *Columbia Journal of Transnational Law*, 23, 56, 1985, pp. 561-576.

> people's socio-legal action alone can call to order these 'out-laws'."[6]

What are the mechanisms that the concerned judiciary adopts to achieve the above objectives ? These may be subdivided under the following categories.

(ii) **The New Pedagogy**

The judges claim new philosophy of justice as the basis of their radical approach. *Judicial activism* is recognized as a patent and a desirable approach. The recently appointed Chief Justice of India who is probably the strongest carrier of this newly emergent culture of public interest litigation, has strongly pleaded for *judicial activism* in an address delivered at the Columbia University School of Law.

> "...The point which I wish to emphasize is that judicial activism is an undeniable feature of the judicial process in a democracy and the only relevant question is what should be the degree and extent of judicial activism permissible to a judge."[7]

Expounding this concept he identifies three varieties of activism : *technical activism* whereby the judges may order to tear the veil of secrecy directing the government to make certain secret documents public, *juristic activism*, which is not concerned merely with the appropriation of increased power, but is concerned as well with the creation of new concepts, irrespective of the purpose which they serve."

For the Indian situation, however, as he says, neither technical nor juristic activism in the above sense is adequate :

> "...Let me make it clear that the objective for which we are trying to use juristic activism is realization of social justice."[8]

6. Krishna Iyer, *op. cit.*, p. 30.
7. Bhagwati, *op. cit.*, 567.
8. *Ibid.*, 567.

(iii) Methodology

The above-pedagogy of judicial activism is sought to be translated into action through the conduit of "public interest litigation"—which then becomes a new methodology. Elaborating on this modality, as being increasingly made use of by the Supreme Court, Bhagwati says :

> "...It (i.e. Supreme Court) has started wielding judicial power in a manner unprecedented in its history of more than thirty years, and through a variety of techniques of juristic activism it has begun *converting much of the constitutional litigation into public interest litigation calculated to bring social justice within the reach of the common man* (emphasis supplied)."[9]

Having taken the 'above' axiomatic position, several related changes become automatic, on the part of judiciary. First of all the disregard of certain rules or procedures, if they impede the realization of the objective :

> "...My root belief is that proper role of a judge is to do justice between the parties before him. If there is any rule of law which impairs the doing of justice, then it is the province of the judge to do all he legitimately can to avoid that rule—or even to change it—so as to do justice in the instant case before him. He need not wait for the legislature to intervene : because that can never be of any help in the instant case. I would emphasize, however, the word 'legitimately'; the judge is himself subject to the law and must abide by it."[10]

Another necessary adjunct of the above methodology is what is recognized as the "epistolary jurisdiction" of the court in treating as petitions some of the simple letters written to a court by an aggrieved being denied his fundamental right, or by a public-spirited individual or an organization, on an issue of general public interest, affecting a group or a class of persons.

---

9. *Ibid.*. 567.
10. Krishna Iyer, *op. cit.*, 12.

"...In such a case, a letter addressed by him to the court can legitimately be regarded as an appropriate proceeding within the meaning of Article 32 of the Constitution". (*Ibid*).

Even earlier, the Supreme Court in *S.P. Gupta* v. *Union of India*, had expressed its resolve in a judgement :

"...The court would, therefore, unhesitatingly and without the slightest qualms of conscience cast aside the technical rules of procedures in the exercise of its dispensing power and treat the letter of the public-minded individual as a petition and act upon it."[11]

In simple jurisprudential terms, it means that

"...*Locus standi* must be liberalized to meet the challenges of the times, *Ubi Jus ibi remedium* must be enlarged to embrace all interests of public minded citizens or organizations with serious concern for conservation of public resources and the direction and correction of public power so as to promote justice in its triune facets."[12]

In some of the recent cases, the Supreme Court has even gone beyond providing the above juristic facilities. It has institutionalized the practice of appointing certain socio-legal commissions of inquiry in certain cases to collect additional information in the public interest and accepted the findings as an evidence. Further, in order to ensure that orders issued by Supreme Court on some of these cases are implemented by the state agencies, the Supreme Court has also appointed monitoring agencies. Note the following once again from Bhagwati.

"...We, therefore, thought that it was necessary to evolve in methodology for securing enforcement of court orders in public

11. S.C.C., p. 210, para 17, cited by Mukhoty, *op. cit.*, p. 5.
12. *Ibid*, p. 4. (i) Hira Lal Zila Parishad, Kanpur, Writ No. 1969-70/81 (SC 1981), reported in U.P.L.B.E.C.; (ii) Rural Litigation and Entitlement Centre, Dehra Dun *v*. State of Uttar Pradesh, Writ No. 8209 (SC 1983), cited in Bhagwati 1984; (iii) Bandhua Mukti Morcha *v*. Union of India, 1984, AIR 802, 816-17.

interest litigation, and, with this end in view, we started appointing monitoring agencies. In a case brought by a journalist for protection of women in police custody, the Supreme Court gave various directives and asked a woman judicial officer to visit the police lockups periodically and to report to the High Courts whether the directives were being carried out."[13]

The euphoria of the above justice—who is now the Chief Justice of India, is really catchy.

> "...There can be no doubt, however, that public interest litigation is one of the most powerful weapons invented by the court for the purpose of delivering distributive justice to disadvantaged groups of people."[14]

THE LAW JOURNALISTS

There is, however, a misplaced self-celebration on the part of higher judiciary that a revolution of public interest litigation is afoot, and it is of their exclusive making.

> "...The Supreme Court, through public interest litigation, has found a new historical basis for the legitimation of judicial power and has acquired a new credibility with the people. This development has been the result of intense social activism on the part of some of the justices of the Supreme Court of India."[15]

True, the flowering of this manner of litigation is contingent upon what fate these cases meet in the court. At the same time, the press has played and is playing no mean role in promoting this genre of professional culture. There are stalwarts in the field of legal journalism like A.G. Noorani, Krishan Mahajan, S. Sahay and J. Anthony, who have hardly left any flaw or blemish of the contemporary Indian Legal System un-exposed. Between them-

---

13. Bhagwati, *op. cit.*, p. 577.
14. *Ibid.*, p. 577.
15. *Ibid.*, p. 578.

selves they have criticized the *procedure* as well as the *substantive* law; the governments' handling of the judiciary; judiciary's manner of interpreting the Constitution—the continuity or discontinuity between the Fundamental rights and the Directive principles, the functioning and formation of benches and the question of discrepancy between the judgements passed by various benches on similar cases; the judges' improper handling of their own bureaucratic staff; the inadequate sharing of the information about the Supreme Court judgements, not only among various benches of the Supreme Court itself but also with various High Courts, resulting in several serious errors of judgement, etc., etc. Among the above mentioned journalists, perhaps the most prolific although in the recent years has been Krishan Mahajan who has been writing almost with incessant regularity, his regular Monday column "Legal Perspectives" for Hindustan Times. Some of his recent features have been concerned not merely with the legal system and their various incogruities, but also with Public Interest Litigation of which he has developed a radical critique. Even though rejoicing in the fact that Supreme Court judges are now responsive to the issues of the public weal he feels that the court is not going far enough. Note the following :

> "...On December 16, 1983, Justice P.N. Bhagwati, R.S. Pathak and A.N. Sen unanimously agreed in the Bhandu Mukti case concerning the bonded stone quarry workers of Faridabad in Haryana, that the Supreme Court has the widest power under the Constitution to grant relief against the violation of Fundamental rights. This judicial declaration, however, brings little cheer to the bonded labourers because of what the three judges failed to do in terms of giving actual relief to the labourers before them. This happened inspite of extensive arguments by counsel for the labourers, Mr. Gobind Mukhoty on the report of the commissioner which had specifically designed measures for both immediate and long term relief."[16]

16. Krishan Mahajan : "A Soft Supreme Court", Hindustan Times.

He is also not merely content that various civil liberties organizations are fighting cases on behalf of some disadvantaged sections, but instead bemoans the fact that they are not creating permanent voting constituencies among these people, by educating them about the relevant law/laws.

> "...It is tragic that no attention has been paid by legal aid and social work agencies to capture political power by creating voting banks of those for whose benefits they proclaim themselves to be working."[17]

In this sense, even the working of strongly motivated marxist agencies fail to produce the adequate cheer in him :

> "...The problem is that marxist social work agencies do not believe in the law or even its use as a strategic input. This proceeds on a vulgarised concept of marxism which describes law as a part of superstructure. They forget that *law also can be seized like a gun from the 'enemy' for use against the 'enemy' itself* (emphasis supplied)."[18]

He also realizes that Public Interest Litigation is doomed to be a middle class concept. This is so because the middle class-drawn judges, middle class professionals—inclusive of lawyers both within and outside various social action agencies, and also the middle class bureaucracy in the courts never realize the necessity of disseminating information about the various laws and judgements among the poor people.[19]

THE SUMMING UP

All this need not lead us to the conclusion that a "revolution"[20] assuredly is afoot in the legal and professional culture and is bound to transform the various inmates of the legal system, the judges and the lawyers, in their orientations towards the clients and

17. Krishan Mahajan, "Social Justice Votes", Hindustan Times, 21-5-84.
18. *Ibid.*
19. "Middle Class PIL", the Hindustan Times, 10-9-1984.
20. Gobinda Mukhoty, "Public Interest Litigation ; A Silent Revolution", Supreme Court Cases, I, 1985.

clients-to-be. Yet, a window is opened on an erstwhile well-fortified wall of convention, *status quo* and *locus standi*. Whether or not the new breeze keeps gushing in would depend upon the entire social ecology—inclusive of its political, professional and economic components. It seems that the present euphoria of expectancy as reflected in the flamboyant utterings of some new-look judges and public-spirited lawyers, is a *mood sui generis*, generated out of a synchronic social responsiveness on the part of certain specific judges and specific lawyers. For such a mood to persist and concretise into a certain cultural form, there are several 'givens' that ought to be present.

First of all, to the extent, lawyers have to make a significant contribution towards the promotion of this culture, they have to have a certain solidarity of ethos and a commonality of purpose. The bar in our society, as we know, is cleft into varied levels of practice—scattered all along the micro-macro continuum of organizational settings, i.e. from district court to Supreme Court through High Court. Practice is also pursued at various other courts which may be viewed as located horizontally to each other, i.e, courts as well as tribunals related to income tax, sales tax and labour cases. All these types of professional practices are not only characterized by distinct conditions and parameters of business supply and procurement, but are also disconnected through lack of any common professional focus, interaction and interchange of views and opinions. There is thus not even a ghost of a chance for all the members of this professional fraternity to share a common perspective—whether on the critique of the legal system or on the relevance of juristic innovations such as public interest litigation, class litigation, etc. There is a variety of "fractures"[21] from which

21. The implicit reference here is to an exciting paper : "The Fractured Profession : Structural impediments to Collective Action by the Australian Legal Profession" By Terence C. Halliday, (Research School of Social Sciences; Working Papers in Sociology : The Australian National University, Canberra, 1980)—In this paper, he deftly explains the relatively lower potentional of the Australian bar as compared to the American Bar, for collective social action in terms of the former's structural fragmentation and lack of overarching solidarity.

the profession here suffers, rendering it virtually impotent for any collective social action. This incapacity becomes all the more acute because of conditions of professional oversupply and a tearing competition among the professional colleagues. "Competition limits solidarity and the capacity for corporate social action."[22]

But, the relative lack of fragmentation in the profession or its "un-fractured" or "less-fractured" character need not of its own lead to its involvement in collective social action, which is contingent upon a distinct value-orientation, emergence of a new concern on the part of the professional fraternity. In this, the profession has a long way to go, especically so, since it is well known not only for its social apathy but also for constantly pursuing a host of unprofessional practices,[23] against which virtually no sanctions are exercised by the professional bodies.[24]

My overview of the legal profession in virtually all the modern societies leads me to believe that a pro-poor or pro-people concern on the part of lawyers has always been an elite affair and never extended to the generality of the bar. Motivation on the part of professional elites in different societies to engage in this activity may have been different in each case. But, in India, at least at the present stage of analysis—which is definitely not final, a relatively elitist section of bar seems to be bothered about it. May be, having achieved material affluence, they now look for popular prestige which they are likely to get in case they appear in the Supreme Court on some important writ petitions, pleading the cause of the

22. Marc Galenter, "Making Law work for the oppressed". *The other side*, vol. III. No. 2, March, 1983, p. 9.

23. See—J.S. Gandhi : *Lawyers and Touts*, Hindustan Publishing Corporation, New Delhi, 1982.
— This practice of 'touting is not the hallmark of profession in India alone. For example, Roman Tomasic and Cedric Bullar in their : LAWYERS AND THEIR WORK, The Law Foundation of New South Wales: Sydney, 1978, have brought out the existence of this practice among the Australian lawyers.

24. How important it is to emphasize that in the making of a lawyer "individual self control" needs to be "supplemented by the formal and informal control of the community of colleagues" (D. Rueschemeyer : Doctors and Lawyers : A comment on the Theory of the Professions". *The Candian Review of Sociology and Anthropology*, I, I, p. 1.

poor and the disadvantaged. To some at least, achieving this may open the portals to important public or state appointments. But, then this is definitely not true of all. There is a definite microscopic core of the profession, however tiny and minisicular to whom professional concern with the public weal is gratificational in a very personal and intimate sense. But, how much difference such stalwarts can make to the perpetuation of this new professional culture ?

The legal system, as well as the social system will increasingly find it difficult to absorb these new compulsions as they gathermore and more momentum.[25] Also, their, translation into reality is directly dependent on the attitude and *goodwill* of the bureaucracy at all levels, which often lies in servitude and subjection to the political elites from the high classes and castes and cannot be so easily commandeered by the rulings from the judiciary. How would then this developing drama achieve its catharsis ? Would the executive pay obeisance to the broadening of judiciary's functional domain or would these *new commandments* issued by judiciary asking the state to rectify its flawed functioning bring the economic and political elite into open revolt? All these glorious uncertainties are better left to be answered by the developments in future. But the fact remains that no normative compulsions *de novo* can be imposed upon the unwilling yet privileged citizenry, especially in a democratic framework. Building of social consensus, however, slow, should therefore be pursued simultaneously to ensure the eventual success of such a revolution—which is professional, legal and social at the same time.

---

25. Yogendra Singh addresses himself to the same question, although in a slightly different fashion in "Legal System, Legitimation and Social Change" in *Essays on Modernization in India*, Manohar Pub., New Delhi, 1979, pp. 135-152.

INDEX